THE
VINTAGE
CHURCH
COOKBOOK

THE VINTAGE CHURCH COOKBOOK

CLASSIC RECIPES FOR FAMILY AND FLOCK

PARRISH RITCHIE

The Countryman Press

A division of W. W. Norton & Company

Independent Publishers Since 1923

Manufacturing through Imago
Book design by Faceout Studio
Production manager: Devon Zahn

The Countryman Press
www.countrymanpress.com

A division of W. W. Norton & Company, Inc.
500 Fifth Avenue, New York, NY 10110
www.wwnorton.com

978-1-68268-425-2 (pbk.)

10 9 8 7 6 5 4 3 2 1

To the loves of my life,

my motivation,

my inspiration,

my boys,

SAM & DEAN

Contents

MAIN DISHES & CASSEROLES

DESSERTS

INTRODUCTION

In my family there is an old church cookbook. It was put together by all the ladies in the congregation including my mom, my grandma, my great-grandma, my great-great-grandma, and my aunt and my great-aunt, and we each have a copy. The pages are filled with recipes handed down through generations. Some of them don't have exact measurements or cook times and you just kind of have to figure it out. Each page has a tip or hint for the "Gracious Virginia Hostess." The covers on our copies are now a little torn and the paper is yellow. The pages with the recipes we use the most are stuck together from sticky hands. Decades after it was first printed, it is still our favorite cookbook and the one we use the most.

I have so many memories of church and of food, they seem to go hand in hand. When we walked into church every Sunday morning all you could smell was strong coffee. Memories of Vacation Bible School taste like butter cookies and fruit punch. In the summer we would have a big festival with activities, and all the ladies baked their best cakes for the cake walk game. When I got old enough, I was so excited to help out in the concession stand passing out hot dogs. There were church ball team picnics with the best hamburgers and desserts you can imagine. There were spaghetti night dinners and potlucks with long folding tables full of food. When I was growing up our church had a soda machine tucked into a little closet, and my uncle and I would sit impatiently through the service with quarters getting hot in our hands just waiting to get an ice-cold cherry coke. I am so glad to have

LIFE~GIVING VITAMINS

Vitamin A: Acceptance

Vitamin B: Belief

Vitamin C: Confession

Vitamin D: Determination

Vitamin E: Endurance

These vitamins are necessary daily for beauty and health.

these memories and to have that cookbook. Whenever I make one of the recipes from it, it brings back memories of those great times and events when those dishes were served.

I am sure many of you have your own church cookbooks. They have a long history in the United States. Since the mid-1800s, long before the age of sharing recipes online, church and community cookbooks, which were often compiled as fundraisers, were a way for the women to share their treasured, time-tested recipes. In addition to my family's, I have collected vintage church cookbooks over the years—some are from my grandma, some I have found at thrift stores and just couldn't bear to leave behind. I love flipping through them. Each one is a little different, and each has a unique blend of classic recipes and some special variations, but you can always feel such a strong sense of community through the pages. The best ones have tips sprinkled throughout. I just love how the indivudal style of each church comes out through the recipes and tips. Being from Virginia, many of the community cookbooks I've been inspired by are Southern, and those ingredients, flavors, and characteristic Southern warmth come through in the recipes and tips.

There are certain recipes that you see over and over in these cookbooks, with slight variations. Think Amish macaroni salad, meatloaf, and buttermilk pie. Others are more unique—when was the last time you saw a recipe for Jell-O spinach salad? One thing they all have in common is that they are hearty recipes meant to be shared. Many of these recipes would be served at church for a potluck or an after-service lunch. A lot of the dishes are economical: everyone likes to save a penny, especially back then. And a lot of them are casseroles. I mean *a lot* of them are casseroles. I think it's because casseroles are so versatile. They can be made for dinner and there's sure to be plenty of leftovers. Plus they travel well, so they're perfect to take to the Sunday potluck or to that new mom who's too exhausted to cook.

As a blogger and recipe developer, I'm all about finding, creating, and sharing the most delicious recipes, and it's so much fun to browse through the pages of these books and discover just what that looked like to those different communities at different times. When I decided to write this book, I wanted to celebrate the tradition of the church cookbook. It meant bringing together some of the best recipes the various books have to offer—as well as some pretty kitchy vintage ones, like that Jell-O salad. Some of the recipes may seem a little retro, but trust me, they are all delicious and stand the test of time. I hope you enjoy these recipes. With them you can rediscover some old classics, find some new and interesting dishes, and give some real vintage favorites a try!

HORS D'OEUVRES

MILLION DOLLAR DIP

Neiman Marcus Dip, otherwise known as Almond Bacon Cheese Spread and Million Dollar Dip, is such a simple dip to have so many names! It originated in the Neiman Marcus department store restaurant in the 1950s and has been a favorite ever since. With bacon, cheese, and almonds it really does taste like a million bucks!

YIELD: 5 SERVINGS

1½ cups mayonnaise

1 cup shredded sharp Cheddar

5 green onions, sliced

⅓ cup sliced almonds

4 slices bacon, cooked and crumbled

Just mix all of the ingredients together and serve. It can be served right away or kept covered in the fridge for up to 3 days to use whenever you need it; it gets better the longer it sits!

TIP Double this recipe! It goes fast and you can use any leftovers as a sandwich spread—yum!

QUICHE LORRAINE

Quiche is such a classic dish, and, while it sounds fancy, it's a cinch to make. Now we mostly see them as a trendy brunch item, but quiche was quite the craze back in the day, served as appetizers or even as dinner with a side salad. I think a small slice of a buttery quiche filled with cheese and bacon is the perfect appetizer. They also travel well to a potluck or to take to a new mom.

YIELD: 8 SERVINGS AS AN APPETIZER OR 4 AS A LIGHT MEAL

1 premade piecrust, unbaked

1 pound bacon, cut into ½-inch pieces and cooked until crispy

2 cups shredded Swiss cheese

¼ cup green onions, chopped

6 large eggs

1 cup heavy cream

½ teaspoon salt

¼ teaspoon black pepper

Preheat the oven to 425°F.

Place the piecrust into a 9-inch pie plate and crimp edges. Prick the bottom and sides of the crust with a fork. Bake for 6 to 8 minutes until lightly browned. Remove the piecrust from the oven and reduce the oven temperature to 350°F.

To the piecrust add the bacon, cheese, and green onions and gently toss together.

Beat together the eggs, cream, salt, and pepper in a medium bowl. Pour the egg mixture into the piecrust. Bake for 35 to 40 minutes until lightly browned and set in the middle.

Cool slightly, cut, and serve!

TIP If you can't find Swiss cheese to shred, you can cut up Swiss slices, which gives you nice melty pockets of cheese. Yum!

WORTH REMEMBERING

If you break an egg on the floor, sprinkle it heavily with salt and leave it alone for 5 to 10 minutes. Sweep the dried egg into the dustpan.

STUFFED MUSHROOMS

Stuffed mushrooms are an elegant, hearty little appetizer that never seems to go out of style. A simple sausage stuffing is a favorite, and no wonder, it is delicious! The Italian sausage goes perfectly with the earthy flavor of the mushroom, and the Parmesan adds that final touch.

YIELD: 2 DOZEN

24 large mushrooms, stems removed	¼ cup Italian bread crumbs
1 pound ground Italian sausage	4 ounces grated Parmesan
	1 teaspoon minced garlic

Preheat the oven to 350°F.

Hollow out each mushroom cap.

Heat a skillet over medium-high heat. Brown the sausage, draining any excess grease.

Stir the bread crumbs, 3 ounces of the Parmesan, and the garlic into sausage mixture. Cook and stir until heated through, 3 to 5 minutes.

Stuff each mushroom cap with the sausage mixture and place on a baking sheet. Bake the mushrooms for 15 minutes. Sprinkle the remaining Parmesan over mushrooms and bake until the top is browned, 2 minutes.

TIP Looking for a pop of spice? Use hot Italian sausage!

SOUTHERN PINEAPPLE SALAD

Oh my, I have come across so many fruit-mayo salads. My grandma confirmed that these used to be all the rage and promises that they can be delicious. This one, made with pineapple rings, is her favorite, but she has made them with different fruits as well. Is there anything more vintage than canned fruit topped with a little mayonnaise and cheese? It sounds like a strange combination, but it is actually really good. And the presentation is gorgeous. So retro!

YIELD: 10 SERVINGS

10 lettuce leaves

1 (20-ounce) can pineapple rings, drained

5 tablespoons mayonnaise

¾ cup shredded Cheddar

¼ cup chopped walnuts

Arrange the lettuce on a platter. Place a drained pineapple ring on each leaf. Place ½ tablespoon of mayonnaise in the middle of each ring. Sprinkle the cheese and walnuts evenly over each dollop of mayonnaise.

TIP You can substitute cottage cheese for the mayonnaise. You can also garnish with a maraschino cherry or sprinkle some pecans over the top.

GRAPE JELLY SMOKIES

This is a three-ingredient recipe—my favorite kind! These appetizers are everyone's favorite at potlucks, and they seem to always be the first to go. Yes, they are a little ol' fashioned and, yes, the ingredients sound a little strange, but—trust me—these are amazing. Serve them at get-togethers and watch them disappear. Don't forget the frilly toothpicks—they have to be the frilly kind!

YIELD: 10-12 APPETIZER PORTIONS OR 8 DINNER PORTIONS

1 (8-ounce) jar grape jelly

1 (12-ounce) jar chili sauce

2 (14-ounce) packages small smoked sausages

Mix the grape jelly and chili sauce together. Put the jelly mixture and sausages in slow cooker. Cook on low for 2 to 3 hours; you are looking for the sausages to be warmed through and the sauce slightly thickened.

You can serve these straight from the slow cooker to keep them warm, but I like serving them in a dish with frilly toothpicks.

TIP In a rush? You can make these on the stovetop in a large skillet over medium-high heat until the sauce has thickened and reduced slightly.

CARAMEL NUT CEREAL MIX

This is a sweet treat I remember my grandma making all the time. It is completely irresistible. She would set out little bowls of this snack mix all over the house when we had church get-togethers (her house was *the* house to be at for those gatherings). This is such an easy treat to make, and it is a great hostess or holiday gift. My grandma shared the recipe for our church cookbook, and we have made it so many times that the page is actually starting to stick to the ones around it from drops of the caramel goodness.

YIELD: 7 CUPS

½ cup dark corn syrup	Pinch of salt
½ cup packed brown sugar	6 cups Cheerios
4 tablespoons (½ stick) butter	1 cup slivered almonds

Preheat the oven to 300°F. Prepare a cookie sheet with cooking spray or foil.

In a pot over medium-high heat, melt together the corn syrup, brown sugar, butter, and salt and heat until it just comes to a bubble then remove from heat.

In a large bowl mix the cereal and nuts. Pour the sugar mixture into the cereal. Stir to combine. Pour onto prepared cookie sheet. Bake for 30 minutes, stirring about twice.

Remove from oven, let cool. Break into pieces and serve.

TIP You can substitute any nuts you like, even a variety mix!

DEVILED CRAB DIP

My mom loves crabs; she eats them almost every weekend when they are in season. And we always have a few crab feasts out by my grandparents' pool every year, where we cover the picnic tables with newspapers and everyone just sits around and picks crabs. It is so fun and a great tradition.

While our favorite way to eat crab is straight from the shell with Old Bay Seasoning stinging our fingers, my mom used to also make deviled crab dip, which she shared in our church cookbook. As I was making it the other day, the aroma from the oven took me right back to when I was little, when she and I would share this incredible dish.

YIELD: 8 SERVINGS

1 cup mayonnaise

2 eggs

2 tablespoons lemon juice

¼ cup milk

1 tablespoon Old Bay Seasoning

1 teaspoon Worcestershire sauce

1 tablespoon hot sauce (optional)

1 tablespoon yellow mustard

1½ pounds imitation crab meat or lump crab meat

6 green onions, sliced

1 cup plain bread crumbs

Paprika for topping

Preheat the oven to 375°F.

In a large bowl whisk together the mayonnaise, eggs, lemon juice, milk, Old Bay Seasoning, Worcestershire sauce, hot sauce, if using, and mustard.

Carefully fold in the crab, green onion, and bread crumbs.

Spread the mixture in a 9-by-13-inch baking dish and sprinkle with paprika. Bake for 30 minutes.

Serve with crackers.

TIP You can use lump crab meat here, but it is much more economical to use imitation crab in this recipe as you are mixing it with quite a few other flavors.

MINI REUBENS

Another forgotten recipe that used to be invited to all the parties, these mini reubens are delicious little bites of perfection for any get-together. My grandma brings these out around the holidays and I'm lucky if I grab one before they are gone! Quick and easy to make, this appetizer is for when you get tired of serving the same old veggie tray. My grandma makes half of these with sauerkraut and half without.

YIELD: 24 PIECES

1 loaf sliced rye cocktail bread (or 6 slices rye bread)

¾ cup Thousand Island dressing

1 (12-ounce) can corned beef

½ cup sauerkraut, drained well

½ pound Swiss cheese slices, quartered

Preheat the oven to 350°F.

Place the cocktail ryes on a cookie sheet in single layer. If using full-sized rye bread, cut each slice into 4 pieces. Evenly distribute the Thousand Island dressing on all 24 pieces.

Spread the corned beef evenly on each slice of rye. Place about ½ tablespoon sauerkraut on top of the corned beef on only 12 ryes (so only 12 of the 24 minis will have sauerkraut). Top all with Swiss cheese. Pop into oven for 5 to 8 minutes just to melt the cheese. Serve!

CLASSIC CHEESE BALL

The classic cheese ball is great for any event. It's one of those recipes that everyone should learn how to perfect. They look so pretty and everyone just loves them. Each cheese ball maker seems to have their own unique recipe, but the base is usually the same. You can enjoy it as is or you can add your own flair to it!

YIELD: 16 SERVINGS

8 ounces cream cheese, softened

1⅓ cups shredded sharp Cheddar

1 green onion, chopped

½ teaspoon Worcestershire sauce

½ teaspoon hot sauce

Pinch of black pepper

⅓ cup pecans, finely chopped

2 tablespoons parsley, finely chopped (optional)

2 slices of bacon, cooked and crumbled (optional)

With a wooden spoon, combine the cream cheese, 1 cup of the Cheddar, green onion, Worcestershire sauce, hot sauce, and pepper together in a large bowl. Place the cream cheese mixture onto a sheet of plastic wrap. Wrap up the mixture and form into a ball, twisting the ends of the plastic wrap to help create a tight ball. Refrigerate for 2 hours or overnight.

When ready to serve, combine the pecans, remaining Cheddar, the parsley, and bacon, if using, on a plate and roll the cheese ball in this mixture, patting it into the ball as you go. Place on a serving plate with crackers and serve!

TIP Make it your own by switching up the cheese or adding additional ingredients, such as green chilies or olives. You can even roll it in almonds, different herbs, or spices!

SHRIMP DIP

This is a family favorite that my grandma has always made from an old church cookbook. She makes this dip for her friends when it's her turn to host bridge and sometimes, when we're lucky, she makes it for us! It's a creamy, flavorful dip studded with baby shrimp. The original recipe calls for canned shrimp, which is what we use, but you can also use frozen baby shrimp that's been thawed.

YIELD: 4–6 SERVINGS

8 ounces cream cheese, softened	¾ teaspoon garlic salt
1 tablespoon mayonnaise	2 green onions, sliced
⅓ cup chili sauce	Juice of 1 lemon
1 (4-ounce) can cocktail shrimp	Paprika for topping
½ teaspoon hot sauce	

It does not get any easier than this: Mix all ingredients together, except the paprika. Top with a sprinkling of paprika and serve with crackers!

TIP This can be made the day before and chilled in the fridge until ready to serve.

WORTH REMEMBERING

For improved texture and flavor when using canned shrimp, soak shrimp for 1 hour in ice water, then drain.

SPINACH ARTICHOKE CUPS

Spinach and artichoke dip will forever be a favorite appetizer. Going through all these church cookbooks, I found at least one variation of this recipe in every book. I saw it as a baked dip, as a cold dip, as a casserole, and as little bite-sized cups. These cups have a special vintage flair and make a very sophisticated hors d'oeuvre without a lot of hard work.

YIELD: 24 CUPS

4 ounces cream cheese, softened

¼ cup sour cream

1½ cups shredded mozzarella

¼ cup grated Parmesan

1 cup canned artichoke hearts, drained and chopped

1 cup frozen spinach, thawed and drained

2 green onions, sliced

2 garlic cloves, minced

24 phyllo dough shells or 4 sheets

Preheat the oven to 375°F. Grease a mini muffin tin with cooking spray.

In a large bowl combine the cream cheese, sour cream, mozzarella, Parmesan, artichokes, spinach, green onions, and garlic.

Place a phyllo shell into each mini muffin tin, or, if working with phyllo sheets, layer the sheets, cut into 24 squares, and place a stack of 4 squares into each mini muffin tin. Spoon 1 tablespoon of the dip into each dough cup. Bake until the pastry is golden, about 15 minutes.

TIP No time to fill the shells? Just bake the spinach mixture in a small baking dish for a great dip!

CRAB PUFFS

Puffs are a staple appetizer and they are usually made with sea-food, whether it's shrimp, salmon, or crab, like these. Not so long ago, every good hostess knew how to make a puff! I think we all should have a good puff recipe under our belt, and that is where these crab puffs come in. Flaky pastry filled with crab meat and cream cheese makes an absolutely divine hors d'oeuvre.

YIELD: 12 LARGE PUFFS OR 16–18 SMALL PUFFS

1 sheet puff pastry dough, thawed

12 ounces lump crab meat

6 ounces cream cheese, softened

2 teaspoons fresh lemon juice

¼ teaspoon garlic salt

2 green onions, chopped

Preheat the oven to 400°F and lightly grease a cookie sheet.

Roll out the puff pastry dough and cut into equal-sized squares. You can cut 12 larger squares for bigger puffs or 16 to 18 smaller ones.

In a large bowl mix together the crab, cream cheese, lemon juice, garlic salt, and green onion.

Fill each pastry square with about 2 tablespoons of the crab mixture. Pinch the edges together in a diamond shape. Place onto the cookie sheet. Bake for 20 minutes. Serve warm.

PEPPER JELLY CREAM CHEESE DIP

This has to be one of my favorite appetizers. I could eat the whole thing by myself! This may be a recipe that until now you could find only in Southern church cookbooks, but the world needs to know about it. I am not sure if putting only two ingredients together counts as a recipe, but cream cheese and pepper jelly make a magical flavor combination that everyone loves. We Southern hostesses always have these two ingredients on hand, so whenever we have an unexpected guest, or when we just want to bring something quick to that after-church lunch, this simple recipe gets the nod.

YIELD: 6 SERVINGS

1 (8-ounce) block cream cheese, softened	½ cup red pepper jelly

Place the cream cheese block on a serving dish. Spoon the pepper jelly over the top. Serve with crackers!

TIP You can also use green pepper jelly if you prefer.

CLASSIC CHEESE PECAN WAFERS

This recipe is one that every good Southern girl learns at a young age, because it is ridiculously easy to make! These wafers are a favorite in our family, and my great-aunt Sherry always makes them around the holidays. They make the perfect little appetizer that is buttery, cheesy, and just melts in your mouth! Some recipes call for chopped nuts in the dough, but I prefer the classic look of a single pecan on top.

YIELD: 30 WAFERS

4 ounces shredded sharp Cheddar	1 cup flour
8 tablespoons (1 stick) unsalted butter, at room temperature	1 teaspoon salt
	30 pecan halves

Place the cheese, butter, flour, and salt in a food processor and blend until a dough is formed.

Divide dough into two equal pieces and roll each piece into about a 1½-inch round log, wrap in plastic wrap, and refrigerate for at least 2 hours until chilled.

Preheat the oven to 350°F. Line two baking sheets with parchment paper.

Unwrap the dough and slice each log into rounds about ¼-inch thick. Place the dough rounds on the prepared baking sheet and gently press a pecan half into the center of each. Bake for about 15 minutes until lightly golden.

Cool completely to serve. You can keep these in an airtight container for up to a week.

TIP You can add a pinch of cayenne to the dough to give it a little kick.

PINEAPPLE SAUSAGE BITES

This might have to go into the too-retro column, but I came across this recipe a few times and for good reason: these are simple, delicious, and pack a flavor punch. A simple sauce helps them become sweet and caramelized in the oven. They are the perfect vintage appetizer.

YIELD: 15–20 SERVINGS

20 ounces canned pineapple chunks in juice, quartered (reserve the juice)

2 pounds kielbasa sausage, sliced into ½-inch pieces

1 tablespoon soy sauce

1 tablespoon sweet chili sauce

1 tablespoon brown sugar

Preheat the oven to 425°F. Line a baking sheet with foil and spray with cooking spray.

Place a piece of pineapple on top of a slice of sausage and stick a toothpick into them. Place bites onto the baking sheet.

Combine remaining ingredients with 1 tablespoon of the reserved pineapple juice and mix to create the glaze. Brush or drizzle the glaze over the tops and sides of bites. Bake for 15 to 20 minutes. Serve!

TIP Make plenty—these go fast! You can prep them ahead of time and glaze just before baking.

PIMENTO CHEESE DEVILED EGGS

Deviled eggs haven't really gone out of style, but in the 1940s and '50s, they were all the rage. They were served as appetizers for card nights, holiday parties, or any get-together. Back then they were a little fancier than the standard picnic fare of today. Several varieties are featured in different church cookbooks, and I decided to go with this pimento cheese version. Let's bring back the fancy deviled egg appetizer!

YIELD: 2 DOZEN

12 large eggs

¼ cup mayonnaise

¾ cup shredded Cheddar

1½ tablespoons pimentos, plus more for garnish if desired

2 teapoons yellow mustard

1 teaspoon Worcestershire sauce

Place the eggs in a large saucepan. Add water to cover and bring to a rolling boil; cook for 1 minute. Cover the pan with a lid, remove from heat, and let stand for 10 minutes. Drain, cool slightly, and peel.

Cut the eggs in half lengthwise; remove the yolks and set aside in a bowl. Add the mayonnaise to the yolks and mash using a fork. Stir in the cheese, pimentos, mustard, and Worcestershire sauce.

Spoon into the egg whites. Garnish with more pimento if desired. Serve and enjoy!

TIP *If* there are leftovers, mash them up into a delicious egg salad for sandwiches!

WORTH REMEMBERING

To cut hard-boiled eggs in smooth slices, dip the knife in water first.

Don't ever discard the water after boiling your eggs. After the water has cooled use it to water your household plants. They will thank you in their own way for the minerals they receive.

OLIVE BREAD

After going through quite a few vintage books, I realized home cooks in the 1950s *loved* using olives in everything. I even saw some Jell-O recipes with olives! This olive bread has that retro flair but is a little more crowd-pleasing than olive Jell-O. Cheese and lots of black olives come together to make this amazing bread. I love to cut it up and serve as an appetizer, but it would also be a delicious addition to dinner.

YIELD: 16 SLICES

8 tablespoons (1 stick) butter, softened

¼ cup mayonnaise

1 teaspoon garlic powder

2 cups shredded mozzarella

2 green onions, sliced

¼ cup chopped black olives

¼ cup sliced black olives

1 loaf French bread, halved lengthwise

Preheat the oven to 350°F.

Stir together the butter and mayonnaise until smooth and creamy. Mix in the garlic powder, cheese, onions, and olives. Spread the mixture evenly over French bread halves and place on a baking sheet. Bake for 10 to 12 minutes.

TIP You can broil the bread for a minute or two to get a super brown top.

HAM PICKLE ROLL-UPS

Vintage recipes never cease to amaze me with their delicious flavor combinations! This is another three-ingredient appetizer. It's an odd blend of ingredients that really work well together. These roll-ups come together in minutes, can be made ahead, and you don't even have to cook them!

YIELD: 8 SERVINGS

4 slices smoked deli ham (not a thin cut)

4 ounces cream cheese, softened

4 dill pickle spears

Using a paper towel, pat dry the ham slices and the pickles.

Spread 1 tablespoon very soft cream cheese on each slice of ham. Place a pickle spear on each slice of ham and roll up. Refrigerate the roll-ups for an hour.

Slice the roll-ups into 1-inch slices. Secure each roll-up with a toothpick and serve!

TIP Jazz these up by using different flavors of cream cheese, such as garlic and herb or jalapeño!

PIMENTO CHEESE SPREAD

This recipe needs no introduction! We all know about the deliciousness of pimento cheese (and if you don't then you need to come to lunch at my house!). It is popular now to put it on burgers and in mac and cheese. But everyone should know how to make a classic pimento cheese spread. It is unbelievably easy to make, and a good Southern hostess would always keep some on hand for unexpected guests. This recipe is a no-frills base that you can fancy up to make your own. This is great with crackers, and it also makes adorable little finger sandwiches!

YIELD: 5 CUPS

1½ cups mayonnaise

1 (4-ounce) jar diced pimentos, drained

1 teaspoon Worcestershire sauce

4 cups shredded Cheddar

Three steps: Mix all the ingredients. Refrigerate for 2 hours to overnight. Serve with crackers.

TIP Add a pinch of cayenne to spice things up or switch out two cups of the Cheddar for shredded pepper Jack.

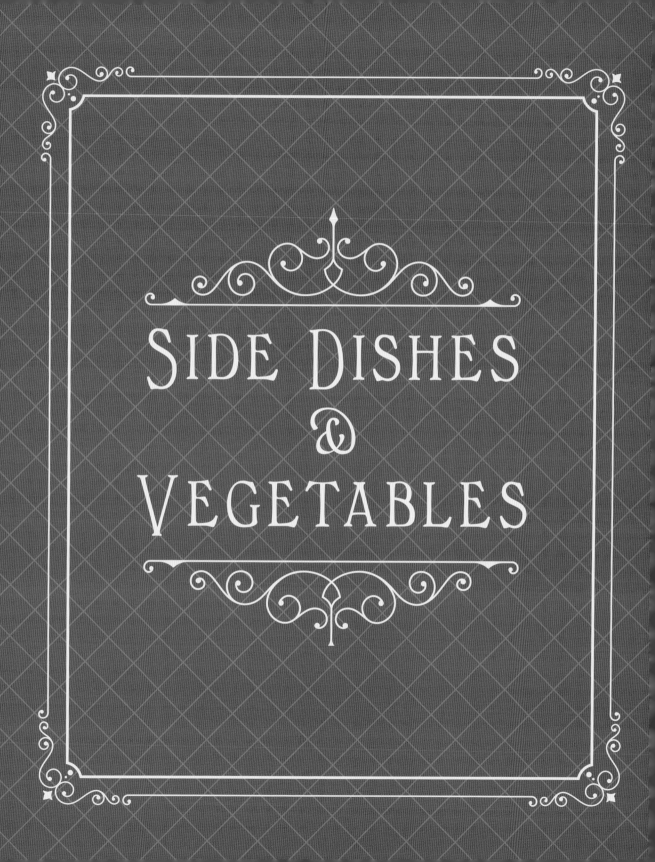

Side Dishes & Vegetables

PINEAPPLE CHEESE CASSEROLE

Okay, now I know some of you might be like, "What?! Pineapple? Cheese? Together in a casserole?!" Believe me, everyone I know who sees this casserole reacts the same way—they just can't fathom how this could ever be good. But then they try a bite and are blown away. It is delicious! This Southern classic is a bit retro, but trust me, it's ridiculously yummy. Please, please, please make this—you will love it, I promise! Did I mention it's topped with buttery cracker crumbs? Oh yes, it creates the most delectable crust.

YIELD: 12 SERVINGS

1 cup sugar

6 tablespoons flour

2 cups shredded sharp Cheddar

1 (20-ounce) can pineapple chunks, drained (reserve the juice)

1 (20-ounce) can crushed pineapple, drained

8 tablespoons (1 stick) butter, melted

1 cup buttery cracker crumbs

Preheat the oven to 350°F. Grease a 9-by-13-inch baking dish.

Stir together the sugar and flour in a large bowl. Mix in the cheese. Add the two cans of drained pineapple and stir until well combined. Pour the mixture into the baking dish.

In a small bowl, add the melted butter, cracker crumbs, and 6 tablespoons of reserved pineapple juice; stir until combined. Spread the cracker mixture on top of the pineapple mixture. Bake for 25 to 30 minutes until golden brown. Cool slightly and serve.

TIP This can also be served at room temperature, and it makes a fabulous potluck dish.

FRIED CABBAGE & POTATOES

This dish is a good old-fashioned, feel-good recipe. And, oh man, is it delicious! I serve it with our fried fish all the time (see page 150), and sometimes I make it for myself for dinner—it is that good! My grandma actually puts all the ingredients in her old white baking dish with the blue flowers on it, and then pops it in the microwave. But I like to cook it on the stovetop and let everything get fried and crispy. Either way you make it, this is a quick and inexpensive side dish that even picky eaters will like!

YIELD: 6 SERVINGS

4 tablespoons (½ stick) butter

1 medium yellow onion, thinly sliced

3 potatoes, thinly sliced

1 head of cabbage, cored and chopped

Salt, to taste

Black pepper, to taste

In a large skillet, melt the butter over medium-high heat. Add the onions and let them cook for 5 to 8 minutes until translucent. Add the potatoes and cook for 15 to 20 minutes, until potatoes and onions are browned.

Remove the potatoes and onions from pan and add the chopped cabbage. Salt and pepper the cabbage and add ¼ cup of water to the pan and cover. Let the cabbage steam until tender, about 20 minutes, adding more water as needed. When the cabbage is tender, take off the lid and let any excess water evaporate.

Return the potatoes and onions to the pan and gently mix. Serve!

TIP If you want to save time, you can use preshredded cabbage.

SEVEN-LAYER SALAD

This classic salad has shown up at just about every church potluck ever. The layers change from person to person. Some people count the dressing as a layer, some people don't. No matter, it is always a hit! This salad travels beautifully, which makes it the perfect potluck dish. It can even be made earlier in the day. Sometimes it is served in a trifle dish, sometimes in a 9-by-13-inch pan, or even in a big old mixing bowl. Whatever you serve it in, make sure it's clear so that everyone can see all the pretty layers!

YIELD: 12 SERVINGS

1 head of lettuce, chopped	1 cup mayonnaise
2 cups broccoli, chopped	¼ cup sugar
1 cucumber, thinly sliced	Pinch of black pepper
1 medium red onion, thinly sliced	2 tablespoons white vinegar
	2 cups shredded Cheddar
4 hard-boiled eggs, peeled and sliced or chopped	1 pound bacon, cooked and crumbled

Evenly layer the lettuce, broccoli, cucumber, onion, and eggs in a large glass bowl or 9-by-13-inch glass dish.

Mix the mayonnaise, sugar, pepper, and vinegar together. Pour the dressing all over the top of the salad. Top with the cheese and bacon.

Serve!

TIP Change it up and use your favorite veggies! I've come across a lot of recipes that call for peas, a variation I can't wait to try.

KRAZY BEANS

1 can green limas or butter beans
3 medium cans pork and beans
1 can kidney beans, drained
4 bacon, fried crispy and
1 hamburger

CALICO BEANS

The recipe for these delicious beans was in my church's cook-book as Krazy Beans, but my grandma calls them Calico Beans, which I like better. Do not confuse these beans with baked beans—these are a whole different thing! They are indeed baked, and the base is indeed pork and beans, but this dish is full of bacon, ground beef, and a sweet sauce. These beans are addictive. I have never been able to make enough—I always bring home an empty dish! I'm going to have to start making a triple batch.

YIELD: 8 SERVINGS

4 strips bacon, chopped

1 small yellow onion, chopped

1 pound ground beef

1 (15-ounce) can pork and beans

1 (15-ounce) can kidney beans, drained

1 (15-ounce) can butter beans, drained

1 (15-ounce) can lima beans, drained

½ cup ketchup

1 cup packed brown sugar

3 tablespoons vinegar

Preheat the oven to 350°F.

Cook the bacon, onion, and ground beef in a large skillet over medium-high heat until browned and cooked through. Drain and set aside.

In a 4-quart casserole dish, mix together the ground beef mix-ture with the remaining ingredients. Cover and bake for 1 hour.

TIP You can also make these in the slow cooker. Just pop the beef mixture and the other ingredients in your slow cooker instead of the oven and keep on low for 2 to 4 hours.

MOM'S FAMOUS ITALIAN PASTA SALAD

This is my mom's pasta salad recipe (well, close to it; she'd kill me if I shared her exact recipe!). She edited our church's cookbook, and of course she included her famous pasta salad. For every get-together, pool party, barbecue, or whatever, she is asked to bring her pasta salad; it is that good! This pasta salad is best made the night before so all the flavors have a chance to get happy with each other.

YIELD: 10 SERVINGS

- ½ cup whipped dressing (such as Miracle Whip)
- ½ cup Italian dressing
- 1 tablespoon grated Parmesan
- 4 cups rotini or penne pasta, cooked and drained
- 1 cucumber, peeled and chopped
- 1 small yellow onion, finely diced
- 1 green pepper, chopped
- 1 cup cherry tomatoes, sliced
- 1 tablespoon chopped parsley

Mix the whipped dressing, Italian dressing, and Parmesan together in a large bowl.

Toss in the pasta, cucumber, onion, green pepper, and cherry tomatoes. Gently stir until combined. Top with the parsley.

Refrigerate for at least 2 hours and serve!

TIP If you made this ahead of time and the salad seems to be a little dry, just add a little more Italian dressing before serving.

TOMATO PIE

Another classic Southern dish that everyone should make is tomato pie! This savory pie is a great way to use up all those big ripe summer tomatoes! This dish combines tomatoes, cheese, and basil in a buttery crust for a pie that is out of this world.

YIELD: 8 SLICES

1 (9-inch) premade piecrust, unbaked

3 tomatoes, sliced

Salt

Black pepper

8 fresh basil leaves, chopped

¼ cup chopped green onion

¼ cup mayonnaise

½ cup shredded Cheddar

½ cup shredded mozzarella

Chopped parsley for garnish (optional)

Preheat the oven to 425°F.

Press the piecrust into a 9-inch pie pan; prick the bottom and sides with a fork. Bake the crust until slightly browned, 10 to 12 minutes.

Cool completely. Reduce the oven temperature to 350°F.

Place the tomatoes in a single layer of a colander; sprinkle with salt. Let sit for about 10 minutes to drain.

Arrange a layer of tomatoes in the piecrust. Sprinkle with pepper, some of the basil, and some of the green onions. Continue layering until you get almost to the top of the piecrust.

Mix the mayonnaise with the Cheddar and mozzarella and top the pie with the mixture. Bake until cheese is melted and bubbly, about 30 minutes.

Cool, slice, and serve! Garnish with parsley, if using.

TIP You can add sliced tomatoes to the top for a pretty garnish!

CORN PUDDING

Corn pudding has to be one of my favorite foods on the Thanksgiving or Christmas dinner table. My family usually serves this at the holidays, but it is wonderful year-round and so easy to make. It is slightly sweet, full of whole kernel corn and creamed corn, and it is just utterly delicious! I can't get enough of this stuff.

YIELD: 8 SERVINGS

5 eggs	4 tablespoons cornstarch
8 tablespoons (1 stick) butter, melted	1 (15-ounce) can whole kernel corn, drained
¼ cup sugar	2 (14.75-ounce) cans creamed-style corn
½ cup milk	

Preheat the oven to 400°F. Grease a 2-quart baking dish.

In a large bowl, lightly beat the eggs. Add the melted butter, sugar, and milk. Whisk in the cornstarch. Stir in both the whole kernel corn and creamed corn. Pour the mixture into the prepared baking dish. Bake for 1 hour. Serve!

TIP You can replace the canned whole kernel corn with the same amount of frozen corn if you prefer.

FUNERAL POTATOES

This is a famously delicious dish with an unfortunate name. When there is a funeral here in the South, people bring tons of food (most are potluck-style foods you find in every church cookbook), and after the funeral there is a get-together and everyone eats a ton. Someone will always bring a huge spiral ham adorned with pineapple rings and cherries, and there will always be funeral potatoes. These potatoes are cheesy, hearty, and comforting. Potatoes and cheese are about as comforting as it gets. This recipe also makes a lot and travels well, so it is great for happier occasions too!

YIELD: 10 SERVINGS

12 tablespoons (1½ sticks) butter

1 (2-pound) package frozen, shredded hash brown potatoes, thawed

1 (10.5-ounce) can cream of chicken soup

1 cup sour cream

½ cup finely diced yellow onions

2 cups shredded Cheddar

1 teaspoon salt

¼ teaspoon black pepper

2 cups crushed cornflakes cereal

Preheat the oven to 350°F.

Melt 8 tablespoons of the butter in a medium microwave-safe bowl in the microwave. (You will use this bowl later too.)

In a large bowl, combine the hash browns, melted butter, cream of chicken soup, sour cream, onion, Cheddar, salt, and pepper. Place the mixture in a 9-by-13-inch baking dish.

Add the remaining 4 tablespoons of butter to the same microwave-safe bowl and microwave to melt. Add the cornflakes to the melted butter and stir to combine.

Spread the cornflake mixture over the potato mixture. Bake for 40 minutes.

Serve!

TIP Some recipes call for diced potatoes instead of shredded, and either is fine!

MARINATED CARROT SALAD

This is another slightly strange recipe that is wonderful! My mom loves it and she can be kinda picky. My grandma makes this salad, and I had to dig deep in the old cookbooks to find the recipe. It is a refreshing salad and is something different to bring to your next gathering. It's a nice change from the same old side dishes. This salad should be made a day in advance to give the flavors time to come together.

YIELD: 12 SERVINGS

1 (10.5-ounce) can condensed tomato soup

¼ cup sugar

½ cup white vinegar

¼ cup canola oil

1 teaspoon yellow mustard

1 teaspoon Worcestershire sauce

3 (15-ounce) cans sliced carrots, drained

1 small yellow onion, thinly sliced

½ cup chopped celery

1 green bell pepper, thinly sliced

In a large bowl, mix the tomato soup, sugar, vinegar, oil, mustard, and Worcestershire sauce. Add the carrots, onion, celery, and bell pepper. Toss gently to combine.

Cover and refrigerate overnight.

TIP The longer this salad sits the more flavorful it becomes—perfect for making ahead!

THREE-BEAN SALAD

I am obsessed with this salad. Yes, it is super vintage and not as popular at cookouts as it once was, but let's bring it back! It is delicious, simple to make, and flies off the table once people taste it. I use the three traditional beans—kidney beans, green beans, and wax beans—but you can switch around the beans to include your favorites! Try butter beans or garbanzo beans for a different twist. This is another recipe to make ahead so that the beans can soak up the flavor of the vinaigrette.

YIELD: 16 SERVINGS

¾ cup sugar

⅔ cup white vinegar

⅓ cup vegetable oil

½ teaspoon salt

½ teaspoon black pepper

1 (15-ounce) can green beans, drained

1 (15-ounce) can wax beans, drained

1 (15-ounce) can kidney beans, drained and rinsed

1 stalk of celery, sliced

1 medium red onion, thinly sliced

½ green bell pepper, chopped

In a large bowl, mix together the sugar, vinegar, oil, salt, and pepper, whisking well until sugar is dissolved.

Toss the green beans, wax beans, kidney beans, celery, onion, and green pepper in the vinaigrette.

Let set in the refrigerator for at least 6 hours; overnight is best.

TIP Some recipes call for ¼ teaspoon of celery seed in place of the fresh celery. Either way is delicious!

BROCCOLI CORN BREAD

This is a recipe my family came across in an old cookbook, and it is so good. It quickly became a staple for our Sunday dinners and people fight over the last piece! It has become one of my husband's favorites, and even my kids love it. It makes a ton, so this dish is perfect for potlucks or get-togethers.

YIELD: 12 SERVINGS

2 boxes Jiffy Corn Muffin Mix

2 tablespoons margarine or butter, melted

¼ cup green onions, sliced

4 eggs

2 cups frozen broccoli, thawed and chopped

1 cup cottage cheese

¼ cup milk

Preheat the oven to 350°F. Grease a 9-by-13-inch baking dish.

In a large bowl, mix all of the ingredients until combined. Pour into the prepared baking dish. Bake for 40 to 45 minutes.

Cool and serve!

TIP You can add ½ cup shredded Cheddar to make this a Cheesy Broccoli Corn Bread.

BEST-EVER BAKED BEANS

Baked beans graced every picnic table at our church's ball team picnics. There are still pans of them at every barbecue, cookout, and potluck. They're such a crowd favorite that everyone needs to know how to make great baked beans. I loved the recipes I came across because they all started with pork and beans, and that is the key to making the best baked beans. Also, allowing enough time for them to bake is really important. You want thick baked beans, not soupy ones.

YIELD: 16 SERVINGS

8 slices bacon

1 small yellow onion, finely chopped

2 (28-ounce) cans pork and beans

½ cup barbecue sauce

¼ cup packed brown sugar

1 tablespoon yellow mustard

2 teaspoons Worcestershire sauce

Preheat the oven to 325°F.

Chop two slices of the bacon and brown in a large skillet over medium-high heat. Remove the bacon from the pan and place on a paper towel to drain, reserving the bacon grease in the pan.

Add the onions to the pan with the bacon grease and cook for 5 to 8 minutes until translucent. Add the beans, barbecue sauce, brown sugar, mustard, and Worcestershire to the pan and stir to combine. Stir the cooked bacon into the beans.

Pour the beans into a 9-by-13-inch baking dish. Top with the remaining six slices of bacon. Bake until beans are bubbly, about 2 hours.

TIP You can top with slices of red onion before baking to make a pretty presentation.

AMISH MACARONI SALAD

Amish macaroni salad, or mac salad, as we call it, is completely different than your average pasta salad. It is one of my favorites! It is slightly sweet and full of flavor from red bell peppers, hard-boiled eggs, and sweet relish. This recipe makes a ton, which is good because it disappears fast. This is ideal to make in the summer for barbecues and pool parties, but I also whip up a batch for burger night any time of year.

YIELD: 8 SERVINGS

2 cups elbow macaroni

2 cups whipped dressing (such as Miracle Whip)

3 tablespoons yellow mustard

½ cup sugar

2 tablespoons sweet pickle relish

2¼ teaspoons vinegar

¼ teaspoon salt

Pinch of black pepper

¾ teaspoon celery seed

3 hard-boiled eggs, chopped

1 small yellow onion, chopped

1 red bell pepper, chopped

Paprika for garnish (optional)

Bring a large pot of water to boil over medium-high heat. Cook the macaroni to al dente according to package directions, then drain.

In a large bowl, stir together the dressing, mustard, sugar, relish, vinegar, salt, pepper, and celery seed. Add the eggs, onion, and red pepper. Add the macaroni and toss gently until everything is well combined.

Refrigerate for at least 4 hours before serving. Garnish with paprika, if desired.

TIP You can use bow tie or shell noodles for a different look!

SQUASH CASSEROLE

This squash casserole has a reputation in my family. We love it. It is cheesy and comforting, and it is a great way to use up all that summer squash. We have quite a few picky kids in our family, and throughout the years we have managed to trick them all into eating this "mac and cheese"—half the time the kids didn't even know they were eating veggies!

YIELD: 6 SERVINGS

2 tablespoons butter

1 small yellow onion, chopped

4 yellow summer squash, sliced into rounds

2 eggs

½ cup half-and-half or evaporated milk

1¼ cups shredded Cheddar

½ teaspoon salt

¼ teaspoon black pepper

2 cups cubed white bread

Preheat the oven to 375°F. Grease an 8-inch square baking dish.

In a large skillet, melt butter over medium-high heat. Add the onion and cook for 5 to 8 minutes until translucent. Add the squash to the pan and cook for 5 minutes until just tender and starting to brown. Remove from the heat.

In a large bowl, beat the eggs, then stir in half-and-half, ¾ cup of the cheese, salt, and pepper. Gently stir in the squash mixture and bread cubes.

Pour into the baking dish. Top with the remaining cheese and bake for 30 minutes until browned.

TIP Use sharp Cheddar for a bolder cheese flavor!

SOUTHERN BUTTER BEANS

Okay, settle in for a minute, because I have a lot to say about butter beans, a.k.a. lima beans (see Tip). People turn their nose up at butter beans, just like everyone used to hate Brussels sprouts and kale. Those two ingredients are now super popular and seem to be on every menu, yet poor butter beans still have a bad rap. But trust me, if you make them right, you will have a new favorite!

Butter beans have been a staple in my family forever—we usually have them with fried chicken, rice, and gravy. Yum! I make them at least once a week. They are delicious, creamy, and probably my favorite veggie. After seeing many vintage recipes like Lima Beans in Sour Cream or Lima Bean Au Gratin, I realized I had to share this recipe for Southern Butter Beans. Give butter beans a chance, y'all!

YIELD: 4 SERVINGS

1 chicken bouillon cube	½ teaspoon sugar
2 slices bacon or a chunk of leftover ham	½ teaspoon black pepper
1 teaspoon garlic salt	1 (16-ounce) bag frozen lima beans (baby or Fordhook variety)
½ teaspoon onion powder	

TIP In the South we call these butter beans, but when shopping look for lima beans. In the store, the young green ones will be labeled lima beans and the mature beige ones are labeled as butter beans. Also, canned and frozen are *not* the same. Make sure to get frozen lima beans!

Bring 1 cup of water and the bouillon cube to a boil in a medium pot. Add the remaining ingredients. Stir and bring the pot back up to a boil, cover, and reduce the heat to a low simmer.

Cook for 25 to 30 minutes. Make sure the liquid doesn't get too low; add a little more water if needed. Check for tenderness; if the beans still aren't soft, let them cook longer, checking every 5 minutes. Remove bacon before serving.

CLASSIC POTATO SALAD

Every time there is a lunch after church, there are at least two bowls of potato salad! It is one of my favorite things on the pot-luck table. I love how everyone makes their version a little differently. Each one has its own personality and its own special ingredients. I like a simple, classic potato salad. Full of flavor, this one is perfect for any barbecue, potluck, or luncheon.

YIELD: 12 SERVINGS

3 pounds baking potatoes

1 cup light mayonnaise

2 tablespoons yellow mustard

1 small red onion, thinly sliced

¼ teaspoon salt

¼ teaspoon black pepper

¼ teaspoon celery salt

4 large hard-boiled eggs, chopped

Paprika for garnish

Peel the potatoes, dice into ½-inch cubes, and rinse. Place in a large pot and cover with water. Bring to a boil and boil for 20 minutes or until tender. Drain in a colander.

In a large bowl, mix the mayonnaise, mustard, onion, salt, pepper, and celery salt. Add the potatoes and eggs to the mayonnaise mixture. Stir everything together, slightly smashing some of the chunks. Sprinkle the top with paprika.

Refrigerate for at least 6 hours before serving.

TIP Some recipes call for sweet pickle relish; feel free to add ¼ cup if you prefer!

CHEESY BROCCOLI RICE BAKE

I've found this dish in a few church cookbooks, and I know I have come across it at church lunches and potlucks. Even so, this bake seems to be most popular as a dish to take to someone who has recently had surgery, or to new parents who have no time to cook—it's the go-to dish to take to people who need a little comfort. I can understand why! Creamy rice mixed with melty cheese and that pop of broccoli makes for one comforting, delicious dish! It travels and reheats well, and it can feed quite a few. It is also super easy to make! I make it with dinner quite often, and even my picky eaters love it.

YIELD: 10 SERVINGS

8 tablespoons (1 stick) butter

1 small yellow onion, chopped

2 (10-ounce) packages frozen chopped broccoli

1 (10.5-ounce) can cream of chicken soup

½ cup sour cream

⅓ cup milk

½ teaspoon salt

¼ teaspoon black pepper

2 cups shredded Cheddar

2 cups cooked rice (white or brown)

Preheat the oven to 350°F. Grease a 9-by-13-inch baking dish.

In a large skillet, melt the butter over medium-high heat. Add the onion and cook for 5 to 8 minutes until tender. Add the frozen broccoli and cook until thawed and tender, 10 to 12 minutes.

To the skillet add the cream of chicken soup, sour cream, milk, salt, and pepper. Stir to combine. Add 1½ cups of the cheese and stir to blend. Add in the cooked rice and stir to combine.

Pour into the greased baking dish. Top with the remaining cheese. Bake for 30 minutes until bubbly and cheese is melted. Serve!

TIP You can also top it with some crunchy french-fried onions for an extra layer of flavor!

WALDORF SALAD

This little salad has quite the history. The maître d' of the Waldorf Astoria hotel in New York created this delightful salad more than 100 years ago. You can get the original recipe from *The Cookbook by "Oscar" of the Waldorf.* The original had only three ingredients: apples, celery, and mayonnaise. Throughout the years it has been in many, many cookbooks and has changed a lot, before reverting back to its original recipe, and then changing again. However you make it, you must include its original ingredients. Some versions add grapes, some add raisins, most add nuts. This recipe is the variation I came across most often. Hostesses in the '50s loved serving this in lettuce cups for appetizers!

YIELD: 6 SERVINGS

½ cup mayonnaise

1 tablespoon sugar

1 teaspoon lemon juice

Pinch of salt

3 apples, cored and chopped

½ cup thinly sliced celery

½ cup chopped walnuts

½ cup raisins or red grapes

Lettuce for serving

In a medium bowl, whisk together the mayonnaise, sugar, lemon juice, and salt. Stir in the apples, celery, walnuts, and raisins. Refrigerate until ready to serve.

Serve on lettuce leaves.

TIP My grandma sprinkles on dried cranberries for a pop of color!

SPOON BREAD

Spoon bread is an extremely economical dish, which is probably why it pops up frequently in older cookbooks. Similar to corn bread, spoon bread is made with cornmeal. Unlike corn bread that is cut into squares, spoon bread is a softer set bread that is served with a spoon, hence the name. This is a comforting dish that we love to serve along with beans or chili, though my family often just loves a little bowl of it, steaming hot with plenty of butter (and if you are my grandma, an extra dash of salt!).

YIELD: 6 SERVINGS

¾ cup cornmeal	1 cup milk
1 teaspoon salt	2 large eggs
3 tablespoons melted butter	2 teaspoons baking powder

Preheat the oven to 350°F. Grease an 8-inch square baking dish. Bring 1 cup of water to a boil.

Combine the cornmeal and salt in a medium bowl. Slowly add in the boiling water while whisking out any lumps. Add the melted butter and stir to combine. Let the mixture cool for about 5 minutes.

Gently whisk the milk into the cornmeal mixture.

In a separate bowl, whisk the eggs. Whisk the eggs into the cornmeal mixture along with the baking powder. Whisk well to combine.

Pour into the prepared baking dish. Bake for 35 minutes. Spoon bread will be set and slightly browned on top.

Serve the spoon bread warm topped with butter. Yum!

TIP This dish is best served straight from the oven with lots of butter on top. Some people jazz it up a little by adding corn, bacon, or green chilies to the batter.

CAULIFLOWER IN SAUCE

The women who wrote recipes for their church cookbooks all those years ago really loved sticking vegetables in the microwave and covering them with cheese! Hey, I am not going to knock a quick veggie smothered in a tasty cheese sauce. My grandma would often quick-steam broccoli or cauliflower and spoon a little cheese sauce over the top for a veggie side with dinner. This recipe for cauliflower in sauce has a flavorful cheese sauce that will get even your picky eaters asking for seconds.

YIELD: 4 SERVINGS

1 head cauliflower

¾ cup mayonnaise

½ small yellow onion, grated

1 teaspoon lemon juice

1 tablespoon yellow or Dijon mustard

1 cup shredded Cheddar

Wash and trim the cauliflower but leave whole. Place in a microwave-safe dish with 2 tablespoons of water. Cover with plastic wrap and microwave on high for 7 minutes until fork-tender. Drain the water.

Mix the mayonnaise, onion, lemon juice, mustard, and cheese to combine. Spoon over the cauliflower. Microwave for another 2 to 3 minutes until cheese is melted.

TIP You can also make this recipe with a head of broccoli.

JELL-O SPINACH SALAD

Okay guys, this one is just for fun, but if you want to make it, be my guest. This is an honest-to-goodness recipe that was in my own church's cookbook and it was too . . . interesting not to share. This is so classic retro, from back in the days when a hostess would put anything in Jell-O—from meat to veggies and everything in between. The original recipe did not have measurements for some of the ingredients, so I've done my best to provide measurements that would do justice to the spirit of the original dish. So, here is Jell-O Spinach Salad in all its glory, complete with frozen spinach, lemon Jell-O, and cottage cheese.

YIELD: 8 SERVINGS

1 small package lemon Jell-O

1 (10-ounce) package frozen chopped spinach, thawed and drained

1 tablespoon lemon juice

1 cup cottage cheese

1 cup mayonnaise

½ cup chopped yellow onion

1 cup chopped celery

2 tablespoons pimentos

Cooked apples, cherry tomatoes, or carrot ribbons for garnish

Dissolve Jell-O in 1 cup of hot water.

Add all of the ingredients to the dissolved Jell-O. Pour into a ring mold and chill for 6 hours.

Unmold and fill the center of the Jell-O ring with cooked apples, cherry tomatoes, or carrots.

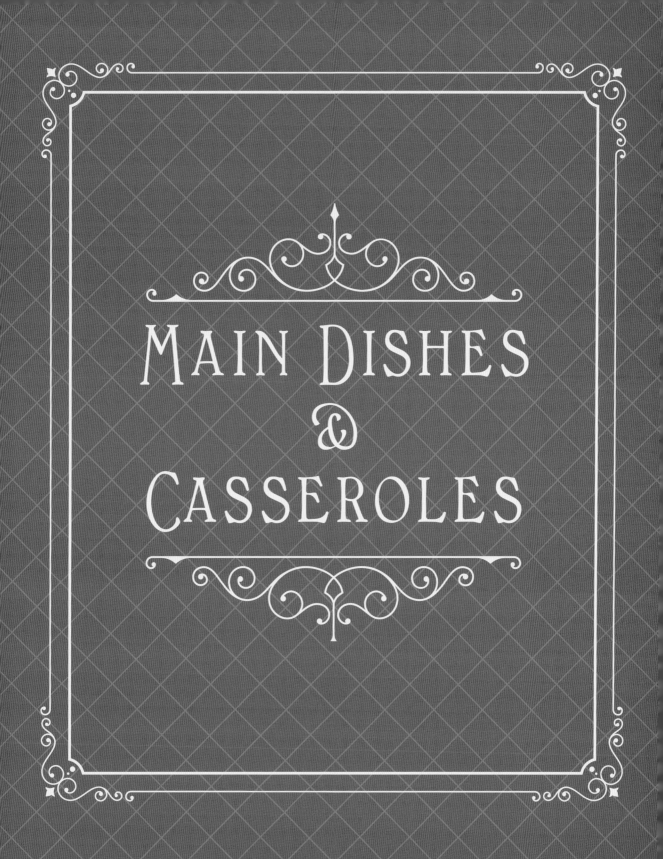

Main Dishes & Casseroles

FRENCH ONION CHICKEN CASSEROLE

This dish is such a simple classic. Like with most casseroles I found in my old church cookbooks, condensed soup plays a big role here. It mixes with chicken and noodles for a simple, crowd-pleasing casserole that you can whip up in minutes! This casserole, which is a perfect way to use up leftover chicken, travels and reheats well, making it great for potlucks!

YIELD: 6 SERVINGS

1 cup shredded Cheddar

½ cup sour cream

½ cup mayonnaise

Pinch of black pepper

1 (10.5-ounce) can cream of mushroom soup

3 cups diced cooked chicken

16 ounces egg noodles, cooked according to package instructions

6 ounces french-fried onions

Preheat the oven to 350°F. Grease a 9-by-13-inch baking dish.

In a large bowl, mix the cheese, sour cream, mayonnaise, pepper, and cream of mushroom soup. Add the chicken and noodles; toss to combine. Spoon into the dish. Bake for 30 minutes.

Sprinkle the fried onions all over the top and cook for another 5 minutes.

Serve!

TIP You can substitute the French onion dip for sour cream for even more flavor!

GOULASH

I have loved goulash ever since I was little. It is a great dish for picky eaters, and it is even better reheated. It is the perfect meal! Goulash is another one of those dishes that everyone has their own take on and adds their own secret ingredients. Some people add Italian seasoning, some people cook the noodles in the sauce, some add them later. My family's version includes green bell pepper and kidney beans, which make it so yummy! Make this recipe for your family and use it as a base to create your own version.

YIELD: 6 SERVINGS

2 tablespoons butter	1 teaspoon sugar
1 large yellow onion, chopped	1 teaspoon salt
1 large green pepper, chopped	½ teaspoon black pepper
2 pounds ground beef	1 teaspoon chili powder
2 garlic cloves, chopped	16 ounces macaroni noodles
2 (15-ounce) cans tomato sauce	1 (15-ounce) can kidney beans, drained
1 (15-ounce) can diced tomatoes	

In a large pot or Dutch oven, melt the butter over medium-high heat and sauté the onion and pepper until just tender, 5 to 8 minutes. Add the ground beef to the pan and cook until browned and no longer pink, 8 to 10 minutes. Drain off any excess grease.

Add the garlic, tomato sauce, diced tomatoes, sugar, salt, pepper, and chili powder and bring to a simmer. Reduce the heat to low and cover with a lid.

In another large pot, bring salted water to a boil for cooking the macaroni. Cook the macaroni noodles until al dente, following package instructions. Drain.

Add the noodles to the meat mixture. Add the kidney beans and gently stir everything together.

Continue to cook over low heat, uncovered for 5 minutes. Serve.

TIP You can top the goulash with shredded cheese and sour cream if you like.

CREAMED POTATOES & CHICKEN

Creamed potatoes is an old Southern dish that you don't see around too often. Sometimes people add ham or chicken to make it a main dish. This recipe for creamed potatoes and chicken is sinfully delicious, and its warmth is perfect on a chilly night. You can also leave out the chicken to create a perfect side dish for any dinner.

YIELD: 4 SERVINGS

4 medium potatoes, peeled and cut into ½-inch cubes

3 tablespoons butter

3 tablespoons flour

1 teaspoon salt

¼ teaspoon black pepper

2 cups milk

1 cup shredded Cheddar

2 cups chopped cooked chicken

Preheat the oven to 350°F. Butter a 3-quart casserole dish.

Place the potatoes in a large saucepan and cover with salted water. Bring to a boil and cook for 10 to 15 minutes until tender. Drain in a colander.

In a medium saucepan, melt the butter over medium heat. Whisk in the flour, salt, and pepper until smooth. Whisk in the milk slowly. Bring to a bubble and cook for 2 minutes until thickened. Stir in the cheese.

Add the potatoes back to their pot and add in the chicken. Gently stir the cream sauce in with the chicken and potatoes.

Place the chicken and potatoes into the prepared casserole dish. Bake for 20 minutes until lightly browned.

TIP This is a great way to use up leftover chicken. You can also add in some cooked bacon, because, well, everything is better with bacon!

NAVY BEAN SOUP

We make a big old ham for every holiday meal, and that means that after every holiday we have a big old pot of Navy Bean Soup. The ham bone makes the perfect base for this rich, flavorful, hearty soup. I get more excited about the soup than the actual ham! A nice slice of buttered corn bread is this soup's best friend and makes for a delicious, comforting meal. (Try the broccoli version on page 76.)

YIELD: 12 SERVINGS

1 pound dried navy beans

1 chicken bouillon cube

1 large yellow onion, chopped

2 garlic cloves, minced

2 ham hocks or 1 ham bone with meat still on it or 1 pound chopped ham

1 (15-ounce) can crushed tomatoes or tomato sauce

1 teaspoon chili powder

1 tablespoon lemon juice

½ teaspoon sugar

½ teaspoon salt

1 teaspoon black pepper

Rinse the beans and discard any debris. Place the beans in a large pot with 8 cups of water and soak overnight (at least 8 hours).

Drain the water from the beans and add 8 cups of fresh water and the chicken bouillon cube, along with the onion, garlic, and ham. Bring to a boil and then reduce heat to low and simmer covered for 2 hours.

Add the tomatoes, chili powder, lemon juice, sugar, salt, and pepper. Simmer for another 30 minutes.

Serve with plenty of freshly baked corn bread!

TIP If you forget to soak your beans overnight, you can quick soak them by rinsing the beans and bringing them to boil in 8 cups of water. Let them boil for 1 minute before removing from heat and letting them soak for 1 hour. Then drain and continue the recipe.

CRANBERRY CHICKEN SALAD CROISSANTS

Does any church ever have a baby shower without chicken salad croissants? I don't think so! They are a staple for every baby shower, bridal shower, or brunch. We go through a lot of chicken salad. We like to add pecans and cranberries to ours, but you can skip those or add your own favorites, such as grapes, almonds, or raisins. I think this chicken salad is best served on a buttery, flaky croissant.

YIELD: 8 SANDWICHES

4 cups chopped cooked chicken

1 tablespoon lemon juice

¼ teaspoon black pepper

½ teaspoon garlic salt

2 stalks celery, chopped

¼ cup dried cranberries

½ cup toasted pecans

1¼ cups good-quality mayonnaise

8 croissants, sliced

Place the chicken in a large mixing bowl. Sprinkle the lemon juice, pepper, and garlic salt all over the chicken. Add the celery, cranberries, and pecans, tossing to combine. Add the mayonnaise and stir until everything is combined. Refrigerate for at least 2 hours.

Place ½ cup of chicken salad on each croissant and serve!

TIP You can use red grapes instead of cranberries, if you prefer.

SLOW COOKER SUNDAY ROAST

Every Sunday we go to my grandparents' house for dinner. My grandma makes all sorts of comforting dinners, like chicken and dumplings, stuffed pasta shells, and her famous fried chicken. Sometimes she makes a roast, which always seems so fitting for Sunday supper because you can throw it all in the slow cooker before you leave for church in the morning. A tender beef roast, slow cooked with onions, carrots, and potatoes, makes its own delicious gravy to spoon over mashed potatoes or egg noodles. It is such a comforting, warming dish that it is usually saved for the colder months. And the sandwiches you get out of it the next day are about as good as the Sunday meal itself!

YIELD: 6 SERVINGS

3 garlic cloves, minced

1 large yellow onion, sliced

3 pounds red potatoes, quartered

6 carrots, peeled and chopped

3 pounds beef chuck roast

1 teaspoon garlic salt

1 teaspoon black pepper

2 (1-ounce) packets brown gravy mix

In the bottom of the slow cooker, place the garlic, onions, potatoes, and carrots. Place the roast on top of the vegetables. Sprinkle the roast with the garlic salt and pepper.

Mix one packet brown gravy mix with 1 cup of water. Pour the gravy over roast. Cover and cook on low for 6 to 8 hours or high for 4 to 6 hours. You'll know the meat is done when it falls apart with a fork.

Plate the vegetables on a serving platter and place the roast on top.

Mix the remaining packet of brown gravy mix in with the drippings from the roast—just stir it into the warm drippings and your gravy is ready!

Serve with egg noodles or mashed potatoes and the extra gravy.

TIP Add frozen pearl onions halfway through the cooking process to give a real vintage look to the finished dish.

FRITO PIE BAKE

When I came across this recipe in my church cookbooks, I knew it would be the perfect dish to serve when my husband's friends come over to play cards. (By cards I mean Dungeons & Dragons, not poker!) This is a simple, crowd-pleasing dish that I also love to make for dinner with salad. It is fast to prepare, my picky eaters love it, and our friends love it too. I mean who doesn't like having chips for dinner?

YIELD: 8 SERVINGS

1 pound lean ground beef

1 small yellow onion, finely chopped

1 (1-ounce) package taco seasoning mix

1 (15-ounce) can tomato sauce

1 (15-ounce) can black beans, drained and rinsed (optional)

1 (9.25-ounce) bag corn chips (about 5 cups)

2 cups shredded Colby Jack or Cheddar

Toppings such as green onions, tomatoes, olives, jalapeños, or sour cream

Heat the oven to 350°F.

In a large skillet, brown the beef and onions over medium-high heat for 8 to 10 minutes until cooked through, drain.

Stir in the seasoning mix with ⅔ cup of water and cook for 5 minutes until bubbling. Reduce the heat to medium and stir in the tomato sauce and beans.

In a 9-by-13-inch baking dish, place a layer of corn chips, then half the meat mixture, then half the cheese. Repeat layers. Bake for 20 minutes until cheese is melted and edges are bubbly.

Top with your favorite toppings and serve!

TIP Use chili cheese or ranch-flavored corn chips for even more flavor!

ROMAN CHICKEN

Roman chicken has quite the history in our family. My grandma loves it, but as a child my mom hated it! We tease my mom about that often, but she's not so much of a picky eater anymore. Now this is everyone's favorite. It is a simple chicken dish with tomato sauce and red peppers baked on top of sliced potatoes and spinach. This dish makes for a perfect, quick weeknight meal served over white rice or even just with a side salad.

YIELD: 4 SERVINGS

1 tablespoon butter or oil

1 medium yellow onion, thinly sliced

1 red bell pepper, sliced

1 (15-ounce) can tomato sauce

2 garlic cloves, minced

½ teaspoon dried oregano

½ teaspoon salt, plus more for sprinkling

¼ teaspoon black pepper, plus more for sprinkling

¼ teaspoon sugar

2 cups frozen chopped spinach, thawed and drained

2 medium potatoes, peeled and sliced

4 boneless, skinless chicken breasts or 6 boneless, skinless thighs

Preheat the oven to 350°F.

In a large skillet, melt the butter over medium-high heat. Add the onion and bell pepper to skillet and cook for 5 to 8 minutes until slightly tender.

Add the tomato sauce, garlic, oregano, salt, pepper, and sugar to the skillet. Let that bubble over medium-low heat while you prepare the rest.

In a 9-by-13-inch baking dish, evenly spread the spinach. Layer the potato slices over the spinach and sprinkle them with salt and pepper. Add the chicken on top of the potatoes. Pour the tomato sauce on top of chicken and cover with foil. Bake for 30 minutes and then remove foil and bake for another 10 minutes.

Serve!

TIP A handful of sliced kalamata olives adds a pop of flavor.

BRUNSWICK STEW

Brunswick stew is a Southern stew that is most common in Georgia and Virginia, and both states claim to be the birthplace of this delicious recipe. Being from Virginia myself, of course, I am biased to believe that it originated here. Either way, this is a fabulous stew that my family usually makes after a cookout as its main ingredients are barbecue chicken, barbecue pork, and corn, all of which we have plenty left over after a barbecue. It also features one of my favorite ingredients: butter beans (lima beans). This stew has a thick, slightly sweet tomato base and is hearty and comforting!

YIELD: 8 SERVINGS

4 tablespoons (½ stick) butter

3 garlic cloves, minced

1 small yellow onion, finely chopped

1 (15-ounce) can tomato sauce

4 cups chicken stock

1 cup barbecue sauce

1 tablespoon Worcestershire sauce

1 tablespoon light brown sugar

2 cups chopped cooked chicken

1 pound smoked pulled pork

2 cups frozen baby lima beans

2 cups frozen or fresh corn kernels

Melt the butter in a large Dutch oven or soup pot over medium-high heat. Add the garlic and onions and sauté until soft.

Stir in the tomato, chicken stock, barbecue sauce, Worcestershire, brown sugar, chicken, smoked pork, lima beans, and corn. Bring the stew to a boil, reduce to a simmer, and cook over low heat until thick and lima beans are tender, about 1 hour, stirring occasionally.

Serve with buttered saltines.

TIP You can substitute the tomato sauce for diced tomatoes if you prefer. This stew also freezes well.

SALISBURY STEAK

When you think of Salisbury steak, you probably think of a foil tray with a side of mashed potatoes and peas that you pull out of the freezer. Before the age of the TV dinner, Salisbury steak was a favorite of housewives everywhere, and people have forgotten that you can make good old classics like this for dinner. Thanks to these old cookbooks, I rediscovered the deliciousness of home-made Salisbury steak in all its glory, and you can too! To keep with tradition, I serve mine with mashed potatoes and peas.

YIELD: 6 SERVINGS

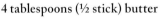

4 tablespoons (½ stick) butter

1 medium yellow onion, sliced

2 pounds ground beef

2 eggs

1 cup bread crumbs

1 tablespoon ketchup

1 tablespoon Worcestershire sauce

1 teaspoon yellow mustard

½ teaspoon garlic salt

1 teaspoon black pepper

2 tablespoons flour

1 (26-ounce) carton beef stock

The gracious Virginia hostess would sprinkle freshly ground nutmeg or chopped fresh mint over buttered peas for a delightful change of taste.

TIP If you would like, you can add mushrooms to the skillet while the onions are cooking.

In a large skillet, melt 1 tablespoon of the butter and start to caramelize the onions over medium heat.

While the onions are softening combine the ground beef, eggs, bread crumbs, ketchup, Worcestershire, mustard, garlic salt, and pepper in a medium bowl and form into six equal oval patties.

When onions are translucent and starting to turn golden, remove them from the skillet. Add another 1 tablespoon butter, melt, then add the beef patties. Cook for 4 to 6 minutes over medium heat until brown and flip to cook the other side for 4 to 6 minutes. Once patties are cooked all the way through, remove them from skillet.

Add the remaining 2 tablespoons of butter to the skillet and melt. Then whisk in 2 tablespoons of flour. Pour in the stock and whisk until bubbly and thickened. Add the onions, and then patties, spooning sauce and onions over the top. Let all simmer together for 10 minutes.

Serve over mashed potatoes for an ultra retro meal.

CLASSIC TUNA NOODLE CASSEROLE

Whoa! Before you skip over this recipe, give this classic tuna noodle casserole a chance! Yes, it's a retro dish. Yes, it's not everyone's favorite. But give it a try! This recipe gives the casserole some flavor and crunch. My whole family loves tuna noodle casserole (except for my brother; we've given up trying). Add caramelized onion to the mix and crunchy french-fried onions on top to give this classic dish the pop of flavor and texture it needs.

Now this might sound strange, but everyone in my family serves this tuna noodle casserole the same way, with peas and blueberry muffins. Trust me! Something about the combination of this casserole, sweet peas, and blueberry muffins make one amazing dinner. I have even converted my husband—he will no longer eat a tuna noodle casserole without a buttered blueberry muffin!

YIELD: 6 SERVINGS

2 tablespoons butter

½ small yellow onion, finely chopped

8 ounces wide egg noodles

2 (5-ounce) cans tuna fish in water, drained well

1 (10.5-ounce) can cream of chicken soup

1 cup french-fried onions

Preheat the oven to 350°F. Butter a 9-by-13-inch baking dish.

In a small pan, melt the butter and caramelize the onion until golden brown and sweet, 8 to 10 minutes.

Boil the noodles in a large pot in salted water, according to package instructions, and drain.

In a large bowl, mix the cooked onion, tuna fish, and cream of chicken soup. Toss in the hot egg noodles and stir to combine.

Pour into the prepared baking dish. Top with french-fried onions and bake for 30 minutes.

Serve with peas and blueberry muffins!

TIP You can substitute the egg noodles for any short noodles you like.

SHEPHERD'S PIE

Oh shepherd's pie, such a classic dish full of comfort! This recipe is in every church cookbook I have ever read, and it's there for good reason—it's delicious. It is a staple on our menu, something I have been eating my whole life. I have seen people try to make it fancy, but shepherd's pie is not meant to be fancy. It is just a hearty, simple, comforting dish. Shepherd's pie is like an old worn snuggly quilt—pure warm, familiar comfort. I've found that this dish is a great way to use up leftover mashed potatoes and veggies, and even my picky kids love it (minus the veggies . . .).

YIELD: 4–6 SERVINGS

1 pound ground beef

2 cups mixed vegetables (corn, peas, carrots, or whatever mix you like)

1 (10.5-ounce) can cream of chicken soup

2 cups mashed potatoes

2 cups shredded Cheddar

Preheat the oven to 350°F.

Brown the ground beef in a large skillet over medium-high heat, 10 to 12 minutes or until cooked through, and drain off the grease. To the ground beef, add the mixed vegetables and cream of chicken soup.

In a 9-by-13-inch casserole dish, layer the meat mixture on the bottom. Top the meat layer with mashed potatoes. Sprinkle all the Cheddar evenly over the top. Bake for 20 to 25 minutes.

Serve!

TIP You can easily substitute ground turkey for the ground beef. If you have picky eaters, you can leave out the vegetables, and then serve it on top of cooked mixed veggies for those who prefer them.

STUFFED CABBAGE ROLLS

These stuffed cabbage rolls are a classic with seasoned beef and rice rolled up in cabbage leaves and then baked in tomato sauce until tender. They are delicious and great over mashed potatoes, egg noodles, or rice.

YIELD: 4 SERVINGS

6 cabbage leaves (see Tip)

1 cup cooked rice

¼ cup grated yellow onion

1 large egg, lightly beaten

¼ cup milk

½ teaspoon salt

¼ teaspoon black pepper

1 pound lean ground beef (85–90% lean)

1 (15-ounce) can tomato sauce

1 tablespoon brown sugar

1 teaspoon Worcestershire sauce

Preheat the oven to 350°F.

Boil the cabbage leaves in a large pan with salted boiling water for 5 to 10 minutes until tender.

Drain and cool while making the filling.

In a large bowl, combine the rice, onion, egg, milk, salt, pepper, and ground beef. Mix until well combined.

Place about ¼ cup of the beef mixture on each cabbage leaf. Give the leaves one roll, pull in the sides, and roll until all rolled up. Place rolls in 9-by-13-inch baking dish seam side down.

Mix the tomato sauce, sugar, and Worcestershire sauce together and pour over rolls. Cover with foil and bake for 1½ hours.

Serve over rice, mashed potatoes, or egg noodles. Yum!

TIP To remove the cabbage leaves more easily, you can either freeze the whole head of cabbage or boil the whole head for about 6 minutes. Don't let the rest of that cabbage go to waste; use it to make Fried Cabbage & Potatoes (page 59).

COLA CRANBERRY-GLAZED HAM

My family loves a sweet ham—honey ham, brown sugar ham, big ham with pineapple rings—the sweeter the better around here. I've seen quite a few recipes for cola-glazed hams in vintage cookbooks. And it's not unusual in the South to add soda to our ham glazes. But this recipe for Cola Cranberry–Glazed Ham has to be our favorite! The cranberry adds a slightly tart pop that works so well with the ham and the sweetness of the glaze. It all comes together in one magical, perfect recipe. This is our favorite for the holidays and goes perfectly with Funeral Potatoes (page 71)!

YIELD: 6–8 SERVINGS

1 cup cola soda

1 cup cranberry sauce

1 tablespoon of your favorite mustard

1 tablespoon brown sugar

5–8 pounds boneless or spiral-cut precooked ham

Preheat the oven to 350°F.

Mix together the cola, cranberry sauce, mustard, and brown sugar until smooth.

Place the ham in a 9-by-13-inch baking dish and coat with half the glaze. Bake for 15 to 20 minutes per pound.

Meanwhile, in a saucepan over medium heat, reduce the remaining glaze until it thickens slightly, 10 to 12 minutes.

Slice the ham and serve with extra glaze.

TIP You can add ½ cup crushed pineapple to the mix for an even sweeter glaze. Yum!

CHEESY CHICKEN & RICE COMFORT CASSEROLE

Every old-school church cookbook I've read has had a cheesy chicken and rice casserole in it, and they were all pretty similar. Why mess with a good thing, right? This is just good ol' comfort straight from the oven—a true crowd pleaser. Make it for dinner and everyone is happy. Take it to a potluck and it's gone! I love this dish because it is a great way to use up leftover chicken and cheese. I can also make it really fast using a rotisserie chicken.

YIELD: 6 SERVINGS

1 tablespoon butter

1 small yellow onion, finely chopped

4 cups chopped cooked chicken

2 cups shredded Cheddar

1 (10.5-ounce) can cream of chicken soup

1 cup sour cream

¼ cup milk

2 cups cooked rice

Preheat the oven to 350°F. Grease a 9-by-13-inch baking dish.

In a medium skillet over medium-high heat, melt the butter and add the onion, cooking 5 to 8 minutes until tender.

In a large bowl add the cooked onions, the chicken, 1½ cups of the Cheddar, cream of chicken soup, sour cream, milk, and cooked rice. Gently mix together until combined.

Pour the chicken-rice mixture into the prepared dish. Top with remaining ½ cup cheese and cover with foil. Bake for 30 minutes or until bubbly.

TIP You can substitute your favorite cheese or mix up a few different kinds. For crunch, you can top it with french-fried onions or crushed croutons during the last few minutes of baking.

BEEF STROGANOFF

Beef stroganoff is a classic dish for sure. It is creamy, beefy, hearty, and comforting. It traditionally calls for stew beef, but in one cookbook I found a version using ground beef—it's a more affordable alternative to stew beef and it comes together in no time. This stroganoff is simple to make, inexpensive, and can feed a crowd, all while tasting amazingly delicious!

YIELD: 4 SERVINGS

2 tablespoons butter

1 small yellow onion, chopped

1 garlic clove, minced

1 pound ground beef

1 teaspoon salt

Pinch of black pepper

1 (10.5-ounce) can cream of mushroom soup

1 cup sour cream

16 ounces egg noodles (or other short pasta)

Put a large pot of salted water on to boil.

In a large skillet, melt the butter and sauté the onion over medium-high heat for 8 to 10 minutes. Add the garlic and ground beef to the pan and brown for 8 to 10 minutes until cooked through. Drain any excess grease.

To the beef-onion mixture, add the salt, pepper, cream of mushroom soup, and sour cream. Let those simmer on low while you boil the noodles.

Boil the noodles in the salted water, following package directions, until al dente.

Toss the noodles with the beef mixture and serve!

TIP You can add canned mushrooms to this dish along with the soup, or you can sauté fresh mushrooms to add.

SOUR CREAM NOODLE BAKE

I could eat my weight in this stuff! It is a creamy, comforting, cheesy dish of love. A true crowd pleaser, it is a potluck favorite and only tastes better the next day. It is also pretty inexpensive to make, which is always a plus in my book. Casseroles like this are extremely popular in old church cookbooks and this one is a true winner!

YIELD: 6 SERVINGS

1 pound ground beef	16 ounces extra-wide egg noodles
1 (15-ounce) can tomato sauce	¾ cup sour cream
½ teaspoon salt, plus more for pasta water	1½ cups small curd cottage cheese
¼ teaspoon sugar	3 green onions, sliced
Pinch of black pepper	2 cups shredded sharp Cheddar

Preheat the oven to 350°F. Bring a large pot of salted water to a boil.

In a large skillet over medium-high heat, brown ground beef for 8 to 10 minutes until browned and no longer pink. Drain.

Add the tomato sauce, salt, sugar, and pepper to taste. Simmer on low.

Boil egg noodles to al dente. Drain.

In a large bowl, combine sour cream, cottage cheese, green onions, and hot noodles and toss to combine.

In a 9-by-13-inch baking dish, spread half the noodle mixture, then half the meat mixture, then half the cheese, and repeat. Bake for 20 minutes, until bubbly and cheese is melted.

TIP I love prepping this in the morning, popping it in the refrigerator, and baking it up for dinner later. It gets better as it rests!

DIXIE PORK CHOPS

These pork chops are so tender and so full of flavor. They are lightly browned before baking with vinegar, sugar, and apples to create the most delectable pork chops ever! If you are a fan of the apple-pork chop combo, then this recipe will be right up your alley. It is amazing served alongside roasted sweet potatoes!

YIELD: 6 SERVINGS

2 tablespoons oil

8 boneless pork chops (can use bone in as well)

½ teaspoon salt

½ teaspoon dried sage

4 apples, cored and sliced

¼ cup packed brown sugar

2 tablespoons flour

1 tablespoon vinegar

½ cup raisins

Preheat the oven to 350°F.

Add the oil to a large skillet over medium-high heat.

Sprinkle the chops evenly with salt and sage. Brown the pork chops on each side, about 3 minutes per side. Transfer the pork chops to a 2-quart baking dish and top with the apple slices and brown sugar.

Add the flour to the oil in the pan and whisk well over medium heat. Add 1 cup of hot water and vinegar to the pan and whisk until thickened. Add the raisins to sauce and pour over pork chops. Bake uncovered for 1 hour.

TIP You can add a dash of cinnamon to the sauce if you like.

HAM & SCALLOPED POTATOES

Any time I make scalloped potatoes, I am reminded of my younger cousin who always talked about how much he loved "seafood potatoes." The rest of us had no idea what he was talking about until we realized he meant scalloped potatoes and had confused them with "scallop" potatoes!

This recipe for ham and scalloped potatoes is a great way to use up leftover ham, which we always have a ton of because we celebrate every occasion with a big spiral ham. The potatoes are creamy and the ham is smoky—a match made in heaven!

YIELD: 6 SERVINGS

5 tablespoons butter	¼ teaspoon black pepper
¼ cup finely chopped yellow onion	2½ cups milk
3 tablespoons flour	6 medium potatoes, peeled and thinly sliced
1 teaspoon salt	1 pound sliced cooked ham

Preheat the oven to 350°F. Grease a 2-quart casserole dish.

In a medium saucepan, melt 3 tablespoons of the butter over medium heat. Cook the onion in the butter for about 5 minutes until tender. Whisk in the flour, salt, and pepper. Cook until combined and add in the milk. Whisk on medium heat until there are no lumps and it starts to bubble.

Layer the potatoes and ham into the prepared casserole dish. Pour the sauce over the potato-ham mixture. Dot the top with pieces of the remaining 2 tablespoons of butter. Cover with foil and bake for 30 minutes. Uncover and bake for 1 hour.

Let cool slightly before serving.

TIP You can sprinkle the top with Cheddar or Parmesan during the last five minutes of baking for a cheesy twist.

FRENCH DRESSING PORK ROAST

While reading through vintage church cookbooks, I discovered that back in the day the one thing people loved cooking with most was salad dressing—even more than canned soup! It's easy to see why; these recipes are delicious. This recipe for French dressing pork roast creates a super tender, super flavorful pork roast with just four ingredients. This has become my go-to for busy days, because I can just throw it all in the slow cooker in the morning, and when I get home it is ready to serve over some white rice. Plus it makes the whole house smell heavenly!

YIELD: 6 SERVINGS

1 (16-ounce) can cranberry sauce

⅓ cup French salad dressing

1 (1-ounce) packet dried onion soup mix

1 (3–4 pound) boneless pork loin roast

In a medium bowl, stir together the cranberry sauce, salad dressing, and onion soup mix.

Place the pork in a slow cooker, and cover with the sauce. Cook on high for 4 hours, or on low for 6 to 8 hours; you can tell the roast is done if it falls apart when you pick it up with a fork.

Serve over rice or roasted potatoes.

(TIP) Nowadays there are a few varieties of French dressing, such as Honey French and Bacon French, so you can switch it up!

HOT CHICKEN SALAD CASSEROLE

This classic luncheon dish is found at many potlucks. It is quick to prepare, full of flavor, and travels well, which makes it the perfect dish to take to an after-church baby shower or evening meeting. It was also a popular dinner item long ago, served over rice or pasta. It has a rich flavor and a nice crunch from the almonds, water chestnuts, and potato chips—yum!

YIELD: 6 SERVINGS

4 cups diced cooked chicken

1 cup chopped celery

1 (8-ounce) can sliced water chestnuts

¾ cup mayonnaise

1 teaspoon lemon juice

½ teaspoon salt

Pinch of black pepper

1 tablespoon grated yellow onion

½ cup shredded Cheddar

1½ cups crushed potato chips

1 cup sliced almonds

Preheat the oven to 350°F. Grease a 9-by-13-inch baking dish.

In a large bowl, mix the chicken, celery, water chestnuts, mayonnaise, lemon juice, salt, pepper, onion, cheese, and almonds.

Pour the mixture into the baking dish and top with the crushed potato chips and almonds. Bake for 30 minutes until bubbly and lightly browned.

Serve over rice or pasta.

TIP You can serve this with crackers as an appetizer!

PORCUPINE MEATBALLS

This is truly a classic dish that is rarely seen anymore, so I was excited to make it again and to introduce it to my family. The name comes from rice being cooked in the meatballs, which then kind of sticks out, giving the meatballs a poke-y appearance. This is a retro-ish dish that holds up to today's standards. The tomato sauce is slightly sweet and tangy, and it is perfect over rice or noodles. Try this one. I promise it will become a family favorite!

YIELD: 4 SERVINGS

1 cup instant white rice, uncooked

½ small yellow onion, finely chopped

1 teaspoon salt

Pinch of black pepper

Pinch of garlic powder

1 pound ground beef

2 tablespoons canola oil

1 (15-ounce) can tomato sauce

2 tablespoons brown sugar

2 teaspoons Worcestershire sauce

In a large bowl, combine ½ cup of water and the instant rice and let sit for a minute. Add the onion, salt, pepper, garlic powder, and beef. Mix well.

Shape into about 24 small (about 1-inch) meatballs and set aside on a baking sheet or tray.

In a large skillet, brown the meatballs in 2 tablespoons oil over medium-high heat. If all of the meatballs do not fit in the pan, you can brown them in two batches. Drain excess oil from pan and return all the meatballs to the pan.

In a large bowl mix the tomato sauce, brown sugar, Worcestershire sauce, and 1 cup of water. Pour over the meatballs.

Reduce the heat; cover and simmer for 30 minutes.

TIP You can substitute ground turkey for the ground beef.

AMISH BAKED CHICKEN

There is nothing I love more than a baked chicken dish. We often just season a cut of chicken and bake it until the skin gets crispy. It's easy-peasy and super yummy. So when I found a recipe for Amish baked chicken, it sounded like something we would like, and indeed, we fell in love! This is so easy to make, and it is perfect for busy weeknights because you can just throw it in the oven while you work on something else. This is another dish that is best over mashed potatoes, rice, or egg noodles, which will soak up all that luscious gravy.

YIELD: 6 SERVINGS

1 cup flour

2 teaspoons garlic salt

2 teaspoons salt

1 teaspoon black pepper

2 teaspoons paprika

6–8 bone-in, skin-on chicken thighs

2 cups heavy whipping cream

Preheat the oven to 350°F.

In a shallow dish or pie pan, mix the flour, garlic salt, salt, pepper, and paprika.

Dredge the chicken pieces in the seasoned flour and place skin side up in a 9-by-13-inch baking dish.

Mix the cream and ½ cup of water in a medium bowl and pour over the chicken. Bake for 1½ hours until the skin is golden brown and crisp.

TIP After cooking, I like to remove the chicken from the pan and give the gravy a good stir while adding a little more salt and pepper as needed. Then I pour the gravy over the chicken and whatever starch we are having with it.

CHICKEN NOODLE CASSEROLE

Every church cookbook has a version of this casserole. It is kind of a clean-out-the-fridge recipe—a great way to use up leftover chicken, veggies, and cheese. It takes minutes to prepare and is a great potluck dish or meal to take to new parents. I really love the cheesy, crunchy cracker topping!

YIELD: 4 SERVINGS

1 (10.5-ounce) can cream of mushroom soup	3 cups cooked medium egg noodles
½ cup milk	¼ teaspoon black pepper
1 cup frozen mixed vegetables	½ cup shredded Cheddar
2 cups chopped cooked chicken	1½ cups crushed buttery crackers

Preheat the oven to 400°F. Grease a 3-quart casserole dish.

In a medium bowl, mix the soup, milk, vegetables, chicken, noodles, and pepper until combined. Pour into the prepared dish. Top with the cheese and crushed crackers.

Bake for 25 minutes or until it is bubbly and the cheese is melty.

TIP You can also use canned vegetables or whichever veggies you have left over in the fridge.

RUSSIAN CHICKEN

This chicken is so moist and so flavorful that it has become one of my kids' favorites! It is quite vintage and oh so delicious. My grandma uses this same sauce to marinate chicken and potatoes for shish-kebabs, it's that good! Russian dressing has become a little harder to find lately, but you can substitute with Catalina dressing. You can also substitute pork chops for the chicken if you want to change it up a bit. This is best served over white rice to soak up all that yummy sauce.

YIELD: 6 SERVINGS

2 teaspoons oil

6 boneless, skinless chicken breasts or 8 thighs

Salt

Black pepper

1 cup Russian dressing (or Catalina dressing)

1 cup apricot jam

1 teaspoon soy sauce (optional)

1 (1-ounce) packet dry onion soup mix

Preheat the oven to 350°F. Heat the oil in a large skillet over medium-high heat.

Salt and pepper the chicken. Add chicken to the skillet and cook for 2 to 3 minutes on each side until browned. Transfer the chicken to a 9-by-13-inch baking dish.

Mix the dressing, jam, soy sauce, and soup mix in a small bowl. Pour over the chicken. Bake for 45 minutes or until the chicken is cooked through.

Serve over fluffy white rice.

TIP You can also make this right in the slow cooker, but I would use thighs instead of breasts to ensure the meat doesn't dry out. Just pop everything in the slow cooker on low for 6 hours or on high for 3 to 4 hours.

FRIDAY FISH FRY

Even outside of Lent, lots of people have fish on Fridays. It's tradition for some people, but then again who wouldn't want crispy fried fish every Friday?

We love fried fish in my family. We like thin white fish dredged in just cornmeal and salt, and then fried—it is delicious. We have it with the Best Hushpuppies Ever (recipe follows) and Fried Cabbage & Potatoes (page 59). It is one of my favorite meals! I could eat it every night. This cornmeal batter is a little different from the beer batter commonly used in restaurants, but trust me, it is the best.

YIELD: 4 SERVINGS

Oil for frying (peanut is best, but you can use vegetable or canola)

2 cups cornmeal

8 tilapia fillets

Salt

Heat about 1 inch of oil to 350°F in large a skillet over medium-high heat. Place a baking rack over a cookie sheet with sides.

Pour the cornmeal in a pie pan or baking dish.

Wet the fish with water. Dredge the fish in cornmeal until completely covered.

Place four pieces of fish at a time in the pan (or however many fit comfortably) and fry for 2 to 4 minutes and flip carefully; cook on second side for 2 to 4 minutes until brown and crispy.

Place on the baking rack to drain oil. Sprinkle with salt to taste as soon as you remove the fish from the pan.

Repeat with the remaining fish.

TIP You can add 1½ teaspoons cajun seasoning to the cornmeal for a pop of flavor.

BEST HUSHPUPPIES EVER

6 cups oil for frying

1½ cups self-rising cornmeal

½ cup self-rising flour

½ teaspoon baking soda

Pinch of sugar

½ teaspoon salt

1 small yellow onion

1 cup milk

1 egg beaten

In a deep heavy pot or the same pan you fried the fish in, preheat the oil for frying to 350°F over medium-high heat. Prepare a plate with paper towels.

In a large mixing bowl, stir together the cornmeal, flour, baking soda, sugar, and salt.

Grate the onion using a box grater and stir it into the cornmeal mixture.

Beat together the milk and egg in a small bowl. Add the milk mixture into the dry ingredients and mix with a wooden spoon until combined.

Drop 1 teaspoon of batter into the oil at a time (they will expand!).

Turn the hushpuppies until golden on all sides.

Drain on the paper towels and serve hot.

SWEET & SOUR BEEF STEW

This is a twist on classic beef stew. Instead of a deep, rich gravy, this stew has a sweet and tangy tomato-based sauce. It is incredibly addictive! This stew cooks in the slow cooker, so it will be ready when you get home. The recipe calls for just carrots, but you can add peas or broccoli, both of which would be delicious in this dish. This Sweet & Sour Beef Stew is best served over rice for an amazing dinner.

YIELD: 6 SERVINGS

3 pounds stew beef

2 tablespoons oil

1 medium yellow onion, chopped

2 cups sliced carrots

1 (15-ounce) can tomato sauce

½ cup packed brown sugar

½ cup vinegar

2 tablespoons Worcestershire sauce

6 tablespoons cornstarch

Brown the stew beef in oil in a large skillet over medium-high heat.

Add the meat to a slow cooker. Next, add the onions and carrots to the slow cooker.

Combine the tomato sauce, brown sugar, vinegar, and Worcestershire sauce together in a small bowl and pour into the slow cooker.

Cook on high for 4 hours or on low for 6 to 8 hours.

When ready to serve, mix ¾ cup of cold water and the cornstarch together and add to the slow cooker. Stir everything together until thickened, about 5 minutes.

Serve over rice.

TIP You can add your favorite frozen vegetables to the slow cooker an hour or so before serving.

COMPANY CHICKEN

This chicken is so easy to make, so delicious, and so flavorful! It is always a hit any time we make it. It's called company chicken because it is the perfect dish to serve to guests—it's very impressive. I guarantee they will be begging for the recipe. My grandma serves it with egg noodles that she tosses with butter in the pan the chicken cooked in. That way, the noodles soak up all that good flavor.

YIELD: 4 SERVINGS

4 boneless, skinless chicken breasts

8 ounces cream cheese with chives, softened

2 tablespoons butter

8 slices bacon

Preheat the oven to 400°F.

Make a small incision lengthwise on the top of each chicken breast. In each slice, stuff a quarter of the cream cheese and top with ½ tablespoon of butter.

Carefully wrap each chicken breast with two slices of bacon. Place in a 9-by-13-inch baking dish. Bake for 30 to 40 minutes until chicken is cooked through and juices run clear.

TIP This dish can be prepared ahead, refrigerated, and then baked just before serving.

SOUR CREAM CHICKEN ENCHILADAS

My family loves enchiladas. We usually use beef, but I found quite a few recipes for chicken and white sauce enchiladas. Now, we have found our new favorite! Chicken, cheese, and green chilies fill soft tortillas before being covered in a luscious white sauce. These enchiladas are truly heaven sent.

YIELD: 6–8 SERVINGS

4 tablespoons (½ stick) butter	3 tablespoons flour
1 small yellow onion, finely chopped	2 cups chicken stock
3 cups shredded cooked chicken	1 cup sour cream
2 (4-ounce) cans diced green chilies	10 taco-sized flour tortillas
	3 cups shredded Monterey Jack

Preheat the oven to 350°F. Grease a 9-by-13-inch baking pan.

In a large skillet, melt 1 tablespoon of the butter over medium-high heat and add the onion. Cook for 5 to 8 minutes until tender.

Add the chicken and one can of green chilies to the pan; stir to combine. Remove from heat.

In a medium saucepan, melt the remaining 3 tablespoons butter, whisk in the flour, and cook for 1 minute. Add the stock and whisk until smooth. Heat over medium heat until thick and bubbly, 5 to 8 minutes. Reduce the heat to low and stir in the sour cream and the remaining can of chilies.

Mix 2 cups of the cheese with the chicken mixture and evenly divide among the tortillas. Roll each tortilla around the filling and place seam side down in the pan.

Pour the sauce over the enchiladas and top with the remaining cheese. Bake for 20 minutes covered and 5 minutes uncovered.

Serve!

TIP You can substitute pepper Jack if you like things really spicy!

BEEF & BEAN BISCUIT CASSEROLE

My mom used to always talk about this casserole my grandma made for dinner. It had ground beef, beans, barbecue sauce, and biscuits, but she could never remember exactly how it was made. We had forgotten all about it until I came across it in an old cookbook. This recipe is easy to make, hearty, and just the perfect meal for a cold night. I am so happy we found it and can share it with you!

YIELD: 6 SERVINGS

1 small yellow onion, chopped	¼ cup packed brown sugar
1 green bell pepper, chopped	3 tablespoons yellow mustard
1 pound ground beef	1½ cups barbecue sauce
1 (28-ounce) can baked beans	1 (8-count) can biscuits

Preheat the oven to 350°F.

In a large ovenproof skillet over medium-high heat, add the onion, bell pepper, and ground beef. Cook for 8 to 10 minutes until beef is browned and no longer pink. Drain excess grease.

Add the beans, sugar, mustard, and barbecue sauce to the skillet. Bring to a bubble.

Arrange the uncooked biscuits on top. Pop into the oven and bake for 20 minutes until biscuits are cooked through and golden.

TIP You can also bake this in a 9-by-13-inch casserole dish.

CHICKEN FRIED STEAK WITH CREAM GRAVY

A true classic! The steak is nice and tender, the crust is crispy, and the cream gravy is perfect over mashed potatoes or white rice.

YIELD: 4 SERVINGS

2 cups plus 6 tablespoons flour

2 teaspoons baking powder

1 teaspoon baking soda

½ teaspoon garlic salt

1½ teaspoons black pepper (more if you prefer)

1¾ teaspoons salt

1½ cups buttermilk

1 egg

1 tablespoon hot sauce

4 beef cube steaks

Oil for frying

1½ cups evaporated milk

2 cups milk

In a shallow 8-inch square baking dish or pie pan, mix 2 cups of the flour with the baking powder, baking soda, garlic salt, 1 teaspoon of the pepper, and ¾ teaspoon of the salt.

In a separate shallow bowl, beat the buttermilk, egg, and hot sauce with a fork until well blended.

Dredge each steak first in the flour, then in the buttermilk, and again in the flour making sure they are completely covered in flour.

Heat about 1½ inches of oil in a deep heavy skillet to 355°F. Place a baking rack over a cookie sheet with sides.

Fry the steaks about 3 to 5 minutes per side until golden brown. Place the fried steaks on a baking rack to drain grease.

Drain all but 6 tablespoons of the oil from the skillet. Over medium-low heat, whisk the remaining 6 tablespoons of flour into the remaining oil in pan. Whisk in the evaporated milk and regular milk, scraping the bottom as you go. Stir in the remaining 1 teaspoon salt and ½ teaspoon pepper. Raise the heat to medium to get the gravy to bubble and thicken for about 5 minutes.

Serve the gravy over the steaks.

TIP You can either spoon the gravy over the steaks or add the steaks into the pan of gravy before serving them over mashed potatoes or rice.

POTLUCK POT PIE

This is the only pot pie I have ever eaten, and it is the only pot pie I will ever eat. This is how I grew up eating pot pie, and to me it is the best! I do not like a pot pie with a piecrust, and after trying this recipe you probably won't either. A recipe from my church, this pot pie has a creamy filling and a buttery biscuit-like topping that is just amazing. Named Potluck Pot Pie because it makes a lot and is easy to transport, it is perfect for those after-church lunches. Try this and you will never go back to piecrust.

YIELD: 8 SERVINGS

3 cups diced cooked chicken

3 cups mixed vegetables (canned or frozen is fine)

1 (10.5-ounce) can cream of chicken soup

1 (10.5-ounce) can cream of celery soup

1 cup chicken stock

Black pepper (optional)

1½ cups baking mix (such as Bisquick)

1½ cups milk

8 tablespoons (1 stick) butter

Preheat the oven to 350°F. Butter a 9-by-13-inch baking dish.

In a large bowl, mix the chicken, vegetables, cream of chicken soup, cream of celery soup, and chicken stock. Sprinkle with the pepper, if using. Pour into the prepared baking dish.

In a large mixing bowl, mix the baking mix and milk until smooth. Pour the baking mix mixture over the chicken filling.

Slice the butter into pats and place all over the top of the pot pie. Place the baking dish on a cookie sheet to catch drips while baking. Bake for 1 hour uncovered until bubbly and top is golden.

TIP You can make this in two 8-inch square pans and eat one now and freeze the other for later!

MILLION DOLLAR SPAGHETTI

This dish is super rich, hence the name. Three kinds of cheese go into this dish and a whole stick of butter—of course it is rich and decadent with those ingredients! It is so crazy good. I have come across this recipe over and over. It is really simple to prepare, and it often makes its way to the church potluck table or even to spaghetti nights alongside a huge salad and plenty of buttered bread.

YIELD: 8 SERVINGS

8 ounces spaghetti	1 cup small curd cottage cheese
1 pound ground beef	8 ounces cream cheese, softened
1 (16-ounce) jar spaghetti sauce	¼ cup sour cream
8 tablespoons (1 stick) butter, sliced	2 cups shredded mozzarella

Preheat the oven to 350°F.

Bring a large pot of lightly salted water to a boil. Cook the spaghetti to al dente, folowing the package instructions. Drain.

In a large skillet over medium-high heat, cook the ground beef for 8 to 10 minutes until browned and cooked through. Drain excess grease. Add the spaghetti sauce and stir to mix.

Place half of the slices of butter in the bottom of a 9-by-13-inch casserole dish. Spread half of the spaghetti into the dish.

Mix the cottage cheese, cream cheese, and sour cream together in a bowl. Spread the cheese mixture over the spaghetti. Layer the rest of the spaghetti over the cheese mixture. Top the spaghetti with the remaining pats of butter. Pour the ground beef mixture over the spaghetti and spread to cover. Top with the shredded mozzarella. Bake for 30 minutes.

TIP Some recipes call for Cheddar; feel free to substitute.

CREAMED CHIPPED BEEF ON TOAST

This recipe can get a bad rap sometimes, but let me tell you something: if you do it right, you will have a scrumptious dish you can enjoy for breakfast, lunch, or dinner. Some people just make a cream sauce and throw in some beef and call it a day. That is not the right way to make this dish. Also, don't go to the deli section and get a little package of lunch meat beef. You have to go to the canned meat section and get dried beef in a glass jar. After you make this dish, wash that little jar and use it as a drinking glass. My grandma had quite the collection of these glasses when I was younger and I loved drinking out of them! Now I am happy to have my own little collection going. But back to the recipe—make creamed chipped beef this way and you will love it!

YIELD: 4 SERVINGS

2 tablespoons bacon grease or butter

1 (2.25-ounce) jar dried beef

2 tablespoons flour

2 cups warm milk

Black pepper

In a large skillet, melt the bacon grease.

Chop the dried beef, add it to the pan, and lightly brown it. Add the flour to the pan and stir into a thickened roux. Add the warm milk and whisk until thickened, about 5 minutes. Add the pepper to taste.

Serve over toast.

TIP You can also serve this over biscuits or on baked potatoes.

CLASSIC MEATLOAF DINNER

Nothing beats a meatloaf dinner, complete with creamy mashed potatoes and buttered peas. It has to be the food equivalent of a hug from your mama. It is the definition of comfort food. Meatloaf doesn't try to be fancy. I usually just mold it into a loaf shape by hand and bake it, but to give it that vintage vibe I sometimes bake it in a ring mold and fill the center with mashed potatoes, which makes a stunning presentation.

YIELD: 8 SERVINGS

2 pounds ground beef

1 small yellow onion, grated

2 eggs, beaten

1½ cups bread crumbs

¼ cup barbecue sauce

1½ teaspoons Worcestershire sauce

½ teaspoon garlic salt

1 tablespoon yellow or Dijon mustard

1 small green bell pepper, sliced

Preheat the oven to 350°F.

In a large bowl, mix the ground beef, onion, eggs, bread crumbs, barbecue sauce, Worcestershire sauce, garlic salt, and mustard until well combined.

In the bottom of a ring mold or bundt pan, lay the green pepper slices and evenly distribute the ¼ cup barbecue sauce. Press the meatloaf mixture into the mold or bundt pan. (As an alternative, you could hand shape the meat into a loaf, top it with the barbecue sauce and the green pepper slices, and bake on a rimmed baking sheet.) Bake for 1 hour.

Cool slightly and unmold.

Fill the center of the meatloaf ring with prepared mashed potatoes and a few peas for color.

SWEDISH MEATBALLS

Long before the Sweden-based Ikea came to America, this vintage dish was popular with entertaining housewives everywhere! Whether you serve them as appetizers or as a comforting dinner over egg noodles, this classic recipe works perfectly as a potluck dish.

YIELD: 4-6 SERVINGS

1 pound breakfast sausage

1 pound ground beef

2 tablespoons grated yellow onion

1 cup bread crumbs

1½ cups milk

½ teaspoon salt, plus more to taste

½ teaspoon black pepper, plus more to taste

2 tablespoons flour

3 cups (24 ounces) beef stock

1 cup sour cream

Mix the sausage, ground beef, onion, bread crumbs, ½ cup of the milk, salt, and pepper together. Form into 1-inch balls and set aside on a plate or tray.

In a large skillet brown meatballs, turning to cook evenly, 1 to 2 minutes per side. Remove the meatballs from the skillet and place on a clean plate or tray while you make the sauce. Drain all but 2 tablespoons grease from skillet.

Add the flour to the skillet and whisk together with grease to form a roux. Once thickened, add in the beef stock and whisk. Once bubbling and thickened, 8 to 10 minutes, add the remaining 1 cup milk, sour cream, and salt and pepper to taste.

Add the meatballs back to the sauce and simmer on low for 10 minutes.

Serve over buttered egg noodles.

TIP Don't skip the sausage! It adds all the flavor you need. You can also freeze the meatballs before cooking to prepare and serve later.

WORTH REMEMBERING

When shaping meatballs, use an ice cream scoop for even, round meatballs.

CHICKEN & STUFFING BAKE

Confession time! I love boxed stuffing mix. I could eat it all year-round, and I do sometimes make it for a quick lunch. So it is no surprise this long-forgotten recipe was my favorite when I was little. It is a very simple recipe and is great for a weeknight meal. Just steam a little broccoli on the side and you've got dinner!

YIELD: 4 SERVINGS

---

1 (6-ounce) package stuffing mix for chicken

4 boneless, skinless chicken breasts

1 (10.5-ounce) can condensed cream of mushroom soup

Pinch of black pepper

⅓ cup sour cream

Preheat the oven to 400°F.

In a large bowl, add 1⅔ cups of hot water to the stuffing mix; stir until moistened.

Place the chicken in a 9-by-13-inch baking dish.

In a separate large bowl, mix the soup, pepper, and sour cream until blended. Pour over the chicken. Top with the stuffing and cover with foil. Bake for 35 minutes covered and for 5 minutes uncovered.

Serve.

TIP You can use cream of chicken or cream of celery soup for a different flavor.

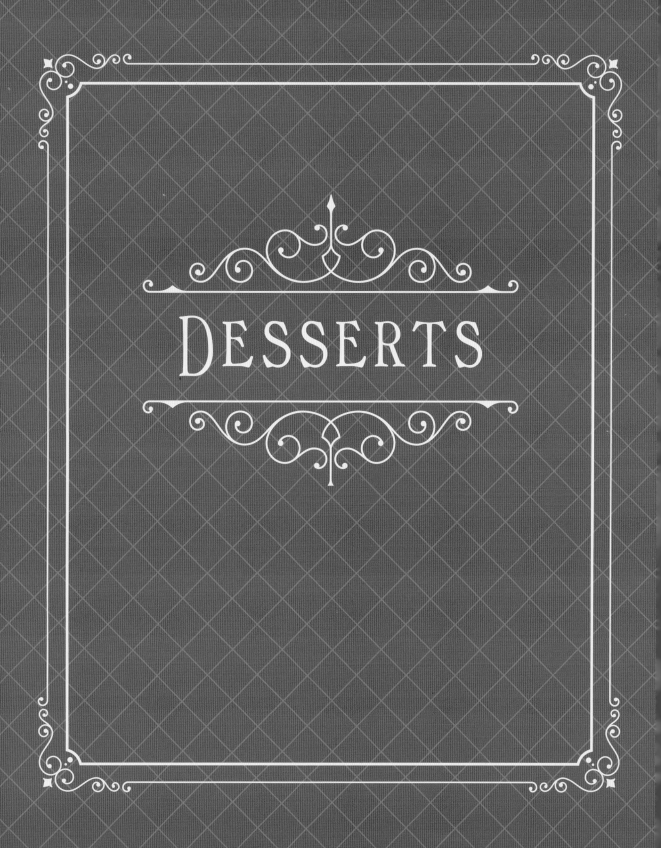

DESSERTS

CLASSIC CARAMEL CAKE

Caramel cake is the perfect dessert for anyone with a sweet tooth. Yellow cake is covered in luscious caramel that keeps the cake moist for days. Caramel cake can be a bit finicky—you have to work quickly with the icing because it can harden up on you real quick. It can also get too thick and start to pull off pieces of the cake. But once you get this baby all iced, you will have one magnificent cake! The icing is to die for. We use my great-grandma's icing recipe, and I just use a boxed yellow cake mix because the caramel is the real star here.

YIELD: 16 SERVINGS

1 (15-ounce) box yellow cake mix

3 eggs

⅓ cup oil

½ pound (2 sticks) butter

¾ cup plus 2 tablespoons evaporated milk (from one 12-ounce can)

4½ cups packed brown sugar

2 teaspoons vanilla extract

Preheat the oven to 350°F. Grease and flour two 9-inch round cake pans.

Combine the cake mix, eggs, oil, and 1 cup of water; mix until incorporated. Divide the batter evenly between the prepared cake pans. Bake for 25 minutes until a toothpick inserted in the middle comes out clean. Cool the cakes for 10 minutes. Turn the cakes out of the pans onto a cooling rack and cool completely.

In a medium saucepan on medium-high heat, combine the butter, milk, sugar, and vanilla extract. Bring to a boil. Stir and turn heat to medium-low so it continues to simmer. Simmer for 7 minutes. Remove from the heat.

Stir the icing until it cools to a spreadable consistency. This will vary; I had to stir mine on and off for about 20 minutes. In cooler weather this time will be shorter.

Place the first layer of the cake on a cake stand. Working quickly, spread some icing on the top of this layer.

WORTH REMEMBERING

When a recipe says "greased pan," grease the pan with solid shortening or an oil, unless butter is specified.

Top with the other cake. Quickly ice the cake with the remaining icing. I find the easiest way is to put a lot of the icing on the top of the cake, let it fall down the sides, and use that to ice the sides. No matter how you ice it, some icing will puddle at the base of the cake. That is okay! It will harden up and become part of that slice and that person will be grateful for the extra caramel.

TIP If your icing gets too hard before you get it all on the cake, you can add a tablespoon of warm evaporated milk to thin it out again.

LIME FREEZE PIE

This is an easy pie that we make a lot in the summer, especially because it is no-bake (besides the crust). It is made with tons of creamy ingredients like cream cheese, Cool Whip, marshmallow fluff, and tart lime sherbet. Just a few hours in the freezer and you have a spectacular pie everyone will love. This recipe makes two pies—and believe me, you will need two because they go fast!

YIELD: 2 PIES, 8 SLICES APIECE

2 (9-inch) premade piecrusts, unbaked

8 ounces cream cheese, softened

1 (7-ounce) jar marshmallow fluff

2 cups lime sherbet, slightly softened

1 (8-ounce) container Cool Whip

Preheat the oven to 350°F.

Poke the piecrusts with a fork and bake for 10 minutes until lightly golden. Let crust cool.

In a large mixing bowl, combine the cream cheese and marshmallow fluff with an electric mixer. Fold in the sherbet and Cool Whip until all are incorporated.

Divide the mixture between the two piecrusts. Place the pies in the freezer for at least 4 hours.

Slice and serve!

TIP You can change the flavor of the sherbet to whichever you like!

PREACHER COOKIES

These cookies are a staple in old church cookbooks. They are said to be called preacher cookies because preachers used to sometimes unexpectedly visit members of their congregation at home, and these cookies were a quick treat that hostesses could make with ingredients they normally had in the pantry. These cookies are quickly whipped up on the stovetop and feature a delicious mix of peanut butter, oatmeal, and chocolate.

YIELD: 18 SERVINGS

8 tablespoons (1 stick) butter or margarine

4 tablespoons unsweetened cocoa powder

2 cups sugar

½ cup milk

Pinch of salt

3 cups quick cooking oats

½ cup creamy peanut butter

1 teaspoon vanilla extract

Mix the butter, cocoa, sugar, milk, and salt together in a large saucepan over medium-high heat. Let boil for 1 minute.

Remove the pan from the stove and stir in the oats, peanut butter, and vanilla.

Drop by tablespoonfuls onto waxed paper. Let cool until hardened and serve!

TIP Use crunchy peanut butter for extra texture!

GRAPE SALAD

Another classic potluck favorite, grape salad is a surprisingly delicious sweet treat. It comes together quickly and can be made the night before. The creamy sauce works perfectly with the pop of the grapes. The whole thing gets topped with brown sugar and pecans. The brown sugar melts into this caramel-like topping. It is easy to see why this is everyone's favorite!

YIELD: 8 SERVINGS

8 ounces cream cheese, softened

1 cup sour cream

½ cup sugar

1 teaspoon vanilla extract

8 cups seedless grapes (red, green, or a combo), washed and dried

2 tablespoons brown sugar

4 ounces chopped pecans

In a large bowl, mix together the softened cream cheese, sour cream, sugar, and vanilla. Stir until the sugar starts to dissolve. Add the grapes and toss lightly until the grapes are coated in cream mixture.

Transfer to a serving dish. Sprinkle with the brown sugar and pecans.

Keep refrigerated.

TIP You can easily skip the nuts. It will be just as delicious!

HUMMINGBIRD CAKE

Hummingbird cake contains no birds; it actually got this name because it is said to be so sweet that it attracts those tiny birds. It is a Southern treat that has been around for ages. The cake is super moist, because the batter includes bananas, oil, and pineapple. It has a hint of cinnamon, a crunch from walnuts, and is always covered in a rich cream cheese frosting. This is a cake traditionally served at Easter lunch but is good any time!

YIELD: 16 SLICES

FOR THE CAKE

3 cups flour

2 cups sugar

1 teaspoon baking soda

1 teaspoon cinnamon

1 teaspoon salt

1½ cups canola or vegetable oil

3 eggs

1 (8-ounce) can crushed pineapple, drained

4 ripe bananas, mashed

1 cup chopped walnuts

FOR THE FROSTING

½ pound (2 sticks) butter, softened

8 ounces cream cheese, softened

1 teaspoon vanilla extract

1 pound powdered sugar

Whole or crushed pecans for garnish

Preheat the oven to 350°F. Grease and flour two 9-inch round cake pans.

Mix together the flour, sugar, baking soda, cinnamon, and salt in a large mixing bowl.

In a separate large bowl, whisk together the oil, eggs, pineapple, bananas, and walnuts. Fold the flour mixture into the wet mixture and stir with a wooden spoon until mixed.

Evenly divide the batter between the two pans. Bake for 25 to 30 minutes or until a toothpick inserted in the center of each pan comes out clean. Cool for 10 minutes and then turn out onto cooling racks. Cool completely.

In a stand mixer or with an electric hand mixer, beat the butter and cream cheese together. Add the vanilla extract. Slowly beat in the powdered sugar until smooth.

Lay one cake layer on a cake plate and spread some frosting on the top of the layer and add the other cake on top. Use the remaining frosting to frost top and sides of cake. Garnish the cake with pecans.

TIP This is a very moist cake, so be sure it cooks all the way in the middle. Checking doneness with a toothpick is imperative.

SHOO FLY PIE

Shoo fly pie is something many of us have heard of, but I don't know if many of us have ever made it. Found in some older cookbooks, this molasses-based pie from Pennsylvania dates to as far back as 1880. I am pretty sure it doesn't get more vintage than this pie! With a strong molasses flavor and crumb top, this unique pie is usually served with coffee.

YIELD: 8 SLICES

1 teaspoon baking soda

1 cup molasses

1 cup flour

⅔ cup packed brown sugar

2 tablespoons butter

1 egg, lightly beaten

1 teaspoon vanilla extract

1 premade piecrust, unbaked

Preheat the oven to 400°F.

Combine ¾ cup of hot water and the baking soda in a medium bowl. Stir in the molasses.

In a separate large bowl, combine the flour and brown sugar. Cut in the butter with a fork until coarse crumbs form. Set aside ½ cup of this mixture.

To the remaining crumb mixture, add the molasses mixture, egg, and vanilla. Beat until well combined.

Pour the mixture into the unbaked piecrust; sprinkle with the reserved crumb mixture. Bake for 10 minutes. Reduce the oven temperature to 350°F. Bake for 35 to 40 minutes or until the filling is set. Cool slightly before serving.

TIP This pie is best served warm with a dollop of whipped cream.

SIMPLE BREAD PUDDING

This is my grandma's bread pudding recipe and it is my favorite. This is a simple bread pudding and that is how we like it. I don't want bread pudding with raisins or one that is made from brioche. I want my bread pudding made with good old white sandwich bread. I don't want a lot of spice or chocolate chips or anything like that in there; I just want a hint of cinnamon and a whisper of lemon. That is what this bread pudding is: a good old wonderful simple bread pudding. I like it best cold from the fridge when I sneak a piece in the middle of the night.

YIELD: 16 SERVINGS

6 eggs	1 teaspoon lemon extract or lemon juice
4 tablespoons (½ stick) butter, melted and cooled	1 teaspoon ground cinnamon
3 cups milk	½ teaspoon salt
¾ cup sugar	12 slices white bread, cut into cubes
2 teaspoons vanilla extract	

Preheat the oven to 375°F. Butter a 9-by-13-inch baking dish.

In a large bowl, whisk together the eggs, butter, milk, sugar, vanilla, lemon, cinnamon, and salt.

Add the bread cubes to the egg mixture and use a spoon to squish all the bread into the egg mixture. Let it sit for about 5 minutes to absorb the liquid.

Pour into the prepared baking dish. Bake for 30 minutes, or until a toothpick inserted into the center comes out clean.

TIP Top with a little whipped cream and a drizzle of caramel if you like.

ICEBOX CAKE

Icebox cake is really just a technique, because you can customize this cake a million ways. It always starts with this simple base of whipped cream and cookies. The cookies and whipped cream are layered and refrigerated overnight, softening the cookies and making this into a cake. Traditionally, chocolate wafer cookies are used. I can't always find those, so instead I use chocolate graham crackers, which work perfectly. You can use any cookie you like and even add fruit or caramel in between the layers. Once you get the technique down, feel free to get creative and make your own custom icebox cake.

YIELD: 16 SERVINGS

3½ cups heavy cream

½ cup powdered sugar

2 teaspoons vanilla extract

25 to 30 chocolate graham crackers or chocolate wafer cookies

In a stand mixer, whip the heavy cream with the powdered sugar and the vanilla extract until stiff peaks form.

In the bottom of a 9-by-13-inch dish, spread a little of the whipped cream. On top of that add a layer of the chocolate graham crackers. Next spread a third of the whipped cream. Another layer of the chocolate graham crackers. Next, half of the remaining whipped cream. Another layer of graham crackers. Then the rest of the whipped cream. Top this with a sprinkle of crushed chocolate graham crackers.

Cover the cake with foil or plastic wrap and refrigerate overnight.

TIP To make this cake even faster, use two containers of Cool Whip instead of making the whipped cream.

NOEL BALLS

These tender shortbread cookies covered in powdered sugar go by quite a few different names, like Russian Tea Cakes, Mexican Wedding Cookies, and Snowballs. In our family we call them Noel Balls. They are our favorite cookies around the holidays, but they are wonderful all year-round. It wouldn't be Christmas without a tin of these on my grandma's table. They melt in your mouth and are irresistible!

YIELD: ABOUT 3 DOZEN

½ pound (2 sticks) butter, softened

½ cup powdered sugar, plus more for rolling

1 teaspoon vanilla extract

2¼ cups flour

¾ cup finely chopped pecans

¼ teaspoon salt

Heat the oven to 400°F.

Mix the butter, ½ cup powdered sugar, and vanilla in a large bowl. Stir in the flour, pecans, and salt until a dough forms. Roll the dough into about 1-inch balls. Place on an ungreased cookie sheet. Bake for 10 to 12 minutes or until set and just lightly golden, *not* brown.

Remove from the cookie sheet and roll hot cookies in the powdered sugar. Place on a cookie rack to cool.

Roll in the powdered sugar again after cooled. Store in an airtight container.

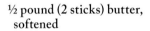 **TIP** You can leave out the nuts, or you can substitute the pecans for walnuts or almonds.

WORTH REMEMBERING

To keep cookies from burning on the bottom, turn the baking pan upside down and bake them on the bottom of the pan. Try it and you will never do it any other way.

PEACH DUMP CAKE

Dump cakes used to be all the rage. Housewives everywhere were thrilled with this delicious cobbler-style cake that could be made with just a few ingredients. Then the dump cake fell off the map. But dump cakes came roaring back a few years ago. My mom used to make a peach dump cake all the time when I was little, and it was so delicious. It is a potluck favorite because it makes a lot and comes together quickly!

YIELD: 16 SERVINGS

2 (16-ounce) cans peaches in heavy syrup

1 (18-ounce) package yellow cake mix

8 tablespoons (1 stick) butter

½ teaspoon cinnamon

Preheat the oven to 375°F.

Empty the peaches into a 9-by-13-inch baking dish. Cover the peaches with the dry cake mix and press down evenly. Cut the butter into thin slices and place all over the top of the cake mix. Sprinkle the cinnamon on top. Bake for 45 minutes.

Serve with vanilla ice cream!

TIP You can switch out the peaches for apple pie filling.

OLD-FASHIONED FUDGE PIE

I know I say every pie recipe in this book is easy, but this one seriously is the easiest. It is one of my favorites because I can make it any time—I always have the ingredients for it on hand. This pie is rich, fudgy, and perfect for chocolate lovers. The hardest part of making this pie is waiting for it to cool!

YIELD: 8 SLICES

1 cup sugar

¼ cup flour

3 tablespoons unsweetened cocoa powder

8 tablespoons (1 stick) butter, melted and cooled

2 eggs

1 teaspoon vanilla extract

1 (9-inch) premade piecrust, unbaked

Preheat the oven to 325°F.

Beat together the sugar, flour, cocoa powder, butter, eggs, and vanilla in a medium bowl. Pour into the unbaked piecrust. Bake for 25 to 30 minutes or until set.

Allow to cool completely before slicing.

TIP We like this pie just as it is with a glass of cold milk, but feel free to put a dollop of whipped cream or berries on top.

WATERGATE SALAD

This salad is a potluck staple. It was originally named Pistachio Pineapple Delight until (as the story goes) an unnamed food editor changed it to Watergate Salad when she printed it in her column. Though a decidedly vintage dessert, it has withstood the test of time and is still popular today. Pistachio pudding mixes with crushed pineapple and marshmallows to create a cool, creamy salad that everyone loves. I love making it because it is so vintage, so retro, and so delicious!

YIELD: 8 SERVINGS

1 (20-ounce) can crushed pineapple in juice, undrained

2 (3.4-ounce) boxes pistachio flavor instant pudding

1 cup mini marshmallows

½ cup chopped pecans

2 cups Cool Whip

In a large bowl, mix the pineapple, pudding, marshmallows, and pecans. Fold in the Cool Whip.

Chill for 1 hour.

Serve!

TIP A maraschino cherry garnish makes this dessert perfect!

BETTER THAN ANYTHING CAKE

I remember my grandma making this cake quite a bit for our church's ball team picnics. This cake is a sinful mix of chocolate cake, caramel sauce, sweetened condensed milk, and whipped topping. The whole thing is finished off with chocolate-covered toffee bits. Keep it in the fridge so that it becomes a cool, creamy, sweet dessert. Using a boxed cake mix makes this cake come together in no time, which is great because the sooner it's ready, the sooner you get to sink your fork into it.

YIELD: 16 SERVINGS

1 (15-ounce) box devil's food chocolate cake mix

3 eggs

⅓ cup vegetable oil

1 (14-ounce) can sweetened condensed milk

1 (16-ounce) jar caramel topping

1 (8-ounce) container Cool Whip

1 (8-ounce) bag chocolate-covered toffee bits

Preheat the oven to 350°F. Grease a 9-by-13-inch baking pan.

Add the cake mix, eggs, oil, and 1 cup of water to a large bowl and mix until combined. Pour into the prepared baking pan. Bake for 25 minutes or until a toothpick inserted comes out clean. Cool for 10 minutes.

Poke the warm cake with the handle of a wooden spoon all over the top. Drizzle the condensed milk evenly over the cake. Drizzle with half of the caramel topping. Cool cake in the refrigerator 2 hours.

Spread Cool Whip all over top of cake. Drizzle with the remaining caramel. Sprinkle with the toffee bits.

Keep in the refrigerator until ready to serve.

TIP You can use butterscotch or hot fudge in place of caramel topping.

STRAWBERRY JELL-O MOLD

I probably could have filled this whole book with nothing but recipes that use Jell-O molds. Vintage cookbooks have a million of them, with everything from vegetables to hot dogs in them! I wanted to include an easy and tasty Jell-O mold recipe that tastes good and looks pretty when it's done. A nonstick Bundt pan is your friend when making this dessert; anything else might give you trouble with sticking (I found that out the hard way). This Jell-O mold treat is full of creamy strawberry goodness!

YIELD: 10 SERVINGS

1 (6-ounce) package strawberry flavor gelatin

1½ cups chopped strawberries

1 (8-ounce) container Cool Whip

WORTH REMEMBERING

Wash fruit-stained hands in lemon juice to remove stains.

Add 1½ cups of boiling water to the gelatin mix in a large bowl and whisk for 2 to 3 minutes until the gelatin is completely dissolved. Stir in 1 cup of cold water. Refrigerate for 30 minutes.

Place the chopped strawberries in a nonstick Bundt pan.

Fold the Cool Whip into the cooled gelatin to combine. Pour the gelatin mixture into the Bundt pan and refrigerate for 4 hours or overnight.

Unmold gently. Serve with more Cool Whip and berries!

TIP You can easily unmold the Jell-O by dipping the bottom of the pan into warm water for about 15 seconds and then turning it over onto a serving platter.

TEXAS SHEET CAKE

This sheet cake is the best potluck dessert you could ever make. It can feed a crowd, and it is super simple to make. It is not the prettiest cake ever, but it sure is tasty and has an out-of-this-world icing that you'll want to eat with a spoon! This cake gets its deep chocolate flavor from boiling the chocolate that goes into the batter and the icing. You can serve this cake right out of the pan, or you can cut it into little squares and serve it in cupcake liners.

YIELD: 16-24 SERVINGS

FOR THE CAKE

2 cups flour

2 cups sugar

¼ teaspoon salt

½ pound (2 sticks) butter

3 tablespoons unsweetened baking cocoa

½ cup buttermilk

1 teaspoon baking soda

1 teaspoon vanilla extract

2 eggs, beaten

FOR THE ICING

8 tablespoons (1 stick) butter

3 tablespoons unsweetened baking cocoa

6 tablespoons milk

2½ cups powdered sugar

1 teaspoon vanilla extract

Preheat the oven to 325°F. Spray a 10½-by-15½-inch baking pan (a jelly roll pan) with cooking spray.

In a large bowl, whisk together the flour, granulated sugar, and salt.

In a medium saucepan over medium-heat, bring 2 sticks butter, 1 cup of water, and 3 tablespoons baking cocoa to a boil. Remove from the heat.

Fold the cocoa mixture into the flour until well combined. Add the buttermilk, baking soda, 1 teaspoon vanilla, and the eggs. Stir until all combined.

Pour the batter evenly into the prepared baking pan. Bake for 25 minutes or until a toothpick inserted comes out clean.

While the cake is baking, prepare the icing: In the same saucepan from earlier over medium heat, bring 1 stick butter, 3 tablespoons baking cocoa, and the milk to a boil. Remove from the heat and whisk in the powdered sugar and 1 teaspoon vanilla until smooth.

Pour the frosting over the hot cake. Cool. Cut into pieces and serve.

TIP You can add ½ cup toasted pecans to the frosting. Or you can sprinkle pecans over half the cake so there's something for everyone!

BUTTERMILK PIE

This pie is not fancy. It does not have chocolate or fruit or fancy icing. It doesn't need all of that. It's simple. It's easy to make. Creamy and custardy with a lightly sweet flavor and just enough tang, this pie is my favorite in the world. It is so easy to make I could do it in my sleep. I always double this recipe because it goes so fast. Keep it in the fridge and everyone in your family will be taking a slice every time they open it. Because this pie takes just 5 minutes to put in the oven, you have no reason not to try it!

YIELD: 8 SLICES

3 eggs

8 tablespoons (1 stick) butter,
  melted and cooled

1½ cups sugar

3 tablespoons flour

1 cup buttermilk

1 teaspoon vanilla extract

1 tablespoon lemon juice

1 (9-inch) premade piecrust,
  unbaked

Preheat the oven to 350°F.

Beat the eggs until frothy. Add the butter, sugar, and flour. Whisk until smooth. Whisk in the buttermilk, vanilla, and lemon juice. Stir to combine. Pour into the pie shell.

Bake for 40 to 50 minutes until center is firm.

TIP I know there is a hack to make buttermilk by putting vinegar into milk, but do not use that trick here. You have to use real buttermilk in this pie!

TRIPLE COCONUT CAKE

This is a classically gorgeous cake that I make for my husband's birthday every year. You get three times the coconut from the coconut milk, coconut cream, and shredded coconut. Yum!

YIELD: 16 SLICES

1 (16-ounce) box white cake mix	8 ounces cream cheese, softened
3 eggs	½ pound (2 sticks) butter, softened
⅓ cup oil	
1 cup coconut milk	¼ cup coconut cream
2 cups sweetened coconut flakes	2 pounds powdered sugar

Preheat the oven to 350°F. Grease and flour two 9-inch round cake pans.

Mix the cake mix, eggs, oil, and coconut milk in a large bowl until combined. Divide the batter evenly between the prepared cake pans. Bake for 25 minutes or until a toothpick inserted in center comes out clean. Cool the cake for 10 minutes, then turn out onto a cooling rack and cool completely.

Meanwhile, toast half of the coconut in a dry nonstick skillet over medium heat until toasted, about 5 minutes. Cool.

In a stand mixer or with an electric hand mixer, whip the cream cheese and butter together. Slowly whip in the coconut cream. Slowly beat in the powdered sugar.

Place the first cake layer on a cake stand and spread frosting on the layer of the cake and top with next layer of cake. Frost the top and sides of the cake with the remaining frosting.

Press the toasted coconut into the bottom half of the cake. Press the untoasted coconut onto the upper half of cake.

Slice and serve.

TIP You can cover the whole cake in untoasted coconut flakes if you prefer.

LEMON LUSH

My grandma and I share a love of lemon desserts, and her recipe for Lemon Lush has been around forever. I remember just loving it when I was younger, and I love it even more now. It has a shortbread base studded with pecans and a creamy layer topped with lemon pudding. This is a dessert that everyone goes crazy for. There are a few different "lush" recipes out there, and they are super popular at potlucks because they are so easy to transport.

YIELD: 16 SERVINGS

¼ cup sugar

8 tablespoons (1 stick) butter, softened

1 cup flour

½ cup crushed pecans

1 cup powdered sugar

8 ounces cream cheese, softened

3 cups Cool Whip

3 cups cold milk

2 (3.4-ounce) packages instant lemon pudding

Preheat the oven to 375°F.

Mix together the sugar, butter, flour, and pecans. Press into bottom of 9-by-13-inch baking dish.

Bake for 15 minutes until lightly golden.

In a large mixing bowl, combine the powdered sugar, cream cheese, and 1 cup of the Cool Whip. Spread this mixture onto the crust while it is still warm.

In another large bowl, mix the milk and instant pudding until thickened, 1 to 2 minutes. Spread on top of the cream cheese mixture. Cover the top with remaining 2 cups of Cool Whip.

Refrigerate for 4 hours.

Slice and serve!

TIP Try using pistachio pudding instead of lemon. Yum!

PIG PICKIN' CAKE

This recipe is really dear to my heart. I have such fond memories of the pig pickin' parties we would have at my grandparents' house with everyone from our church. All my friends from church were there, and we got to swim and watch a huge whole pig roasting. Of course this cake was at every pig pickin' party; that's what it is named for! This moist yellow cake, studded with oranges and topped with the most heavenly frosting made of just Cool Whip and crushed pineapple, is to die for!

YIELD: 12 SERVINGS

1 (15-ounce) box yellow cake mix (I like the kind with pudding added)

3 large eggs

⅓ cup vegetable oil

1 (11-ounce) can mandarin oranges, drained (reserve a few for the garnish)

2 (12-ounce) containers Cool Whip

1 (20-ounce) can crushed pineapple, drained

Preheat the oven to 350°F. Grease and flour two 9-inch round cake pans.

In a large mixing bowl, add the cake mix, eggs, oil, 1 cup of water, and drained mandarin oranges. Mix with an electric mixer until well combined.

Divide the batter between the prepared cake pans. Bake for 22 to 25 minutes or until a toothpick inserted comes out clean. Cool slightly and then remove cakes from pans to cooling racks and cool completely.

In another large bowl, mix the Cool Whip with the drained crushed pineapple.

Place one cake on a cake plate and spread some of the Cool Whip on the top and add the other cake layer on top. Frost the top and sides with the remaining Cool Whip. Garnish with mandarin oranges. Keep this cake in the refrigerator.

TIP This cake also looks gorgeous garnished with maraschino cherries.

PRUNE CAKE

This cake is one my grandma used to make all the time, and I remember it being my uncle's favorite. It is a moist, lightly spiced cake with a thin cream cheese glaze. This cake is made with a secret ingredient . . . baby food! That is the secret to its flavor and incredible texture.

YIELD: 16 SERVINGS

FOR THE CAKE

2 cups sugar

3 eggs

1 cup vegetable oil

2 (4-ounce) jars prune baby food

2 cups flour

2 teaspoons baking powder

1 teaspoon ground cinnamon

1 teaspoon ground cloves

1 cup chopped walnuts (optional)

FOR THE ICING

2 ounces cream cheese, softened

2 tablespoons milk

½ teaspoon vanilla extract

½–¾ cup powdered sugar

Preheat the oven to 325°F. Grease and flour a Bundt pan.

In a large bowl, mix the sugar, eggs, oil, and prune baby food.

In a medium bowl, blend together the flour, baking powder, cinnamon, cloves, and walnuts. Fold the dry ingredients into the wet mixture until all are incorporated. Pour the batter into the prepared Bundt pan. Bake for 1 hour. Cool for 10 minutes and turn out onto a cooling rack. Cool the cake completely.

To make the icing, whisk together in a small bowl the softened cheese, milk, vanilla, and ½ cup powdered sugar. Add more of the powdered sugar if glaze is too thin.

Spoon the glaze over cake.

Serve!

TIP This recipe originally called for plum baby food, which can be hard to find. But if you can find it, feel free to use it.

MARTHA WASHINGTON JETS

The gracious Viriginia hostess would always serve one sweet with cocktails; a tray of petite chocolates is an elegant touch.

These little candies have been around forever. They are truly a vintage treat, and it seems like every old cookbook features a version of this recipe. No one is quite sure where the name originated, but it is speculated they were sold at Martha Washington Candies, a chain store that opened all the way back in the 1890s. Filled with coconut and pecans, these "jets" are an amazing candy. They are super easy to make—you just combine a few ingredients, chill, then dip in chocolate. Voilà, you're a candy maker! You can really impress your guests with these little chocolate treats.

YIELD: 40-50 JETS

2 pounds powdered sugar

1 (14-ounce) can sweetened condensed milk

2 cups flaked coconut, more for sprinkling

8 tablespoons (1 stick) butter, melted and cooled

3 cups chopped pecans

16 ounces melting chocolate

Line a large baking pan or serving tray with parchment paper.

In a large bowl, combine the powdered sugar with the condensed milk, coconut, melted butter, and pecans.

Working quickly, roll the mixture into 1½-inch balls and place on the pan or tray.

Refrigerate until the balls are thoroughly chilled, about 2 hours.

Melt the dipping chocolate in a microwave-safe bowl in 30-second intervals until all melted and smooth.

Carefully dip each ball into the chocolate, gently shaking off the excess and placing back on the tray.

Once all the balls are coated, you can drizzle the extra chocolate over the top and sprinkle with coconut.

Keep refrigerated.

TIP These can be made minus the coconut if you are not a fan, but the yield will be smaller.

Acknowledgments

I want to thank some amazing people who helped make this book possible.

To my husband who kept the house clean and the kids occupied so I could write just one more recipe before dinner. For running to the store for a million forgotten items. For putting me to bed with my reality shows and favorite candy after a long day of cooking and photos. For being my biggest supporter and strongest pillar to lean on. Love you, babe.

To my mom who taught us to never give up no matter what, and that God never gives us more than we can handle.

To my grandma for teaching me so many of these recipes, going through her old cookbooks with me, and brainstorming which recipes would be best.

To the rest of my huge, amazing family for being my other biggest supporters.

To my husband's Dungeons & Dragons crew for being my taste testers.

And of course a huge thank you to Coleman Place Presbyterian Church for the words of kitchen wisdom throughout this book and being such a huge part of my childhood, where my family and I have met lifelong friends and created everlasting memories that will always be with us.

INDEX